Henry W. Colby

Rhymes of the local Philosopher

A bequest to the younger Generation

Henry W. Colby

Rhymes of the local Philosopher
A bequest to the younger Generation

ISBN/EAN: 9783337070694

Printed in Europe, USA, Canada, Australia, Japan

Cover: Foto ©ninafisch / pixelio.de

More available books at **www.hansebooks.com**

Rhymes

OF THE

Local Philosopher.

A BEQUEST TO THE

YOUNGER GENERATION.

TAUNTON, MASS.,
1899.

DAVOL PRINTING HOUSE,

Taunton, Mass.

PREFATORY REMARKS.

This Book so nearly reflects the personality of the Author that he deems it a duty to warn those who may not care to meet him, against studying the contents.

Local Philosophy was not the first title suggested by the writer of the couplets contained in the book, the first instalment being presented under the heading of "Local Lunacy." As the name of the verse seemed to descend as a heritage upon the writer, he evidently narrowly escaped being known as the Local Lunatic, a designation perhaps quite as fitting, but less euphonious to a sensitive ear.

For the many pleasant and friendly words given the first volume, the writer is grateful, and he is certain that the present book is an improvement over its predecessor and is the last of its kind.

H. W. C.

CLASSIFIED
TABLE OF CONTENTS.

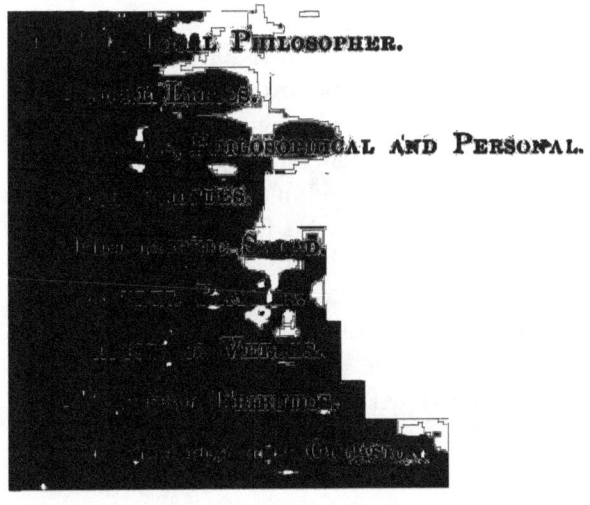

The Local Philosopher

IS INTRODUCED.

Shades of Diogenes in modern guise;
Looking at Truth with half-beclouded ey
No selfish axe to grind, no spoil to seize,
No foe to punish and no friend to please
He draws, by gazing through the lens of
Conclusions less enchanting than exact;
Tearing the veil from Fancy's grand don
Though it may give a fellow-mortal pain
Yet in a kindly way re-decorates
The hours we fain had yielded to our Fates.
Despising shams, he may be often stirred
Into a seeming sharp, ungenerous word,
Yet not unwilling on a soberer thought,
To be with better grace and manners taught.
Does some one tread upon his favorite corn?
He launches forth a thunderbolt of scorn;
Yet doth the grim old fellow in his way,
His debts of gratitude delight to pay;
As doctors, tender even while they kill,
Prefer to slaughter with a sugared pill.

Poor old Philosopher! thyself a sham,
Condemned in many a self-writ epigram,
Preaching to others in thy cynic mood,
How one excels, while one falls short of good;
Pointing for us, with egotistic pride,
A path which doubtless thou hast never tried;
Rasping thy satire, heartless and unkind,
Yet to thine own faults bigoted and blind;
What art thou but a humbug? to reflect
The veriest errors thou wouldst fain correct;
More worthless even in thine own conceit,
Than is the humblest dirt beneath thy feet;
Know that the poor philosophy of Earth
Possesseth but a transitory worth,—
Scarce given life enough or show of power,
To smooth the trials of a passing hour.

Yet doth grim old Diogenes grind on,
Though tongues may wag and critics frown anon,
And if the kindly reader shall discern
Some helpful lesson he may easy learn,—
Some thought which truer peace of mind invokes,
Then his Philosophy is not a hoax.

LOCAL LYRICS.

1—Knotty Walk.

2—The Parson's Ride.

3—Black Jack.

4—Uncle Jim.

5—At Mount Pleasant—(a reverie.)

Knotty Walk.

(A GHOSTLY IDYL.)

I.

Old memories of Knotty Walk,
Could you unseal your lips and talk,
What tales you'd tell, what ghosts would stalk,
(If one such freaks of ghosts believes,)
From 'neath the shadows of your eaves.
I rest me in the barber's chair,
The while the artist clips my hair,
If haply finds he any there,
Which Time has kindly deigned to spare,
(The most being gone, the Lord knows where;)
And, posing thus, my glances fall
Upon the decorated wall
That bounds the said tonsorial hall.
Not all his eloquence of tongue,
In story-telling changes rung,
Or antiquated chestnuts sprung
On guileless ears like mine, and young,
Such as the knight of comb and brush
Is wont our restless moods to hush,

Can quite divert my chastened thought
From off the view mine eyes have sought:
Before me in perspective bold,
A picture of the rare and old,
And, judging by its history told,
Deserving frame of richest gold.
I cast a venerated glance
Upon the old historic manse,
And backward shoots my vision fast
Through divers decades of the past:
A lad, I gazed with curious eye
At relic of the days gone by,
And seemed it but a ruin then,
To me, an urchin less than ten;—
While in each antiquated nook,
It needed but a hasty look
To resurrect some dreaded spook:
Anon as years would glide along,
Less would the ghosts and goblins throng,
And shades with which the spot was rife,
Materialized to real life.
Here, have I heard the gossips say,
A Judge first saw the light of day;
Over yon threshold strode in state
Our Commonwealth's chief magistrate.
Lawyers and doctors here hung out
Their shingles to the folks about;
Tradesmen of every class and craft
Have raked these quarters fore and aft;
The "butcher" and his friend the "baker"
And, very like, the "candle-maker,"

From first to last, have played their part
Within this ancient work of art
Transformed into a business mart.

II.

Within the building's northern wing,
Did Uncle Sam his mailbags bring,
When correspondence, then unpaid,
Was thin as circus lemonade.
No wrapper with adhesive glue,
Or postal stamp in red or blue,
Connived to send a message through.
Only a common foolscap sheet,
Enfolded any way but neat,
The edges with a wafer stuck,
If he who did it had good luck;—
This rude epistle, crudely mailed,
Sometimes went through and sometimes failed,
And if by chance the letter came,
It cost ten cents to bag the game.

III.

Near to the Postal Service site,
Our memory lets in the light
Upon one Barnes, a harness-wright.
Now Barnes had been a soldier bold,
In war with Mexico enrolled,

Before the days of Boys in Blue
And when old veterans were few.
What wonder that the urchin's sight
Should be transfigured with delight,
As in his sanctum-walls we crept
Where his accoutrements were kept;
For in his shop with proper pride
Were hung his trophies, side by side,—
To our admiring gaze a sign
Of heroism quite divine.
With Barnes the first and Barnes the second,
(For here must Barnes's son be reckoned
As one who gave his strength and life
To flatten out rebellious strife,)—
With Sammy Breck, another name
Still living on the roll of fame,
Whose "dad" expounded common law
To those who felt its dreaded paw;—
With these and other sons of Mars
Who gathered glory in the wars,
And some of whom have earned their stars,
Old Knotty Walk has made a score
That patriot hearts may not ignore.

IV.

Among the patriarchs of old
Whose memory is not quite cold,
My thought reflects a worthy pair
Who lived and flourished then and there.

Old "Daddy" Wilson—"J."—I think
His prefix was when dipped in ink;
Likewise his spouse, called "Ma'am" for short,
When courtesy was faintly taught;
Two of the so-called "bucket drops"
That swell the flood of earth's vast crops.
Now Daddy Wilson, in a way,
Was quite important for his day.
The picture we are prone to draw,
Would find him filing some old saw,
Relieving razors from a flaw,
Repairing scissors, tempering knives,
(Thus also tempering fretful wives)
And doing all the thousand things
That bear the name of tinkerings.
An odd old man, serenely bald,
Who often found his glasses stalled
So high up on his cocoanut,
His eyes might quite as well be shut.
But Daddy Wilson had a Dame
Who quite outshone her lord in fame;
Who deftly steered a huckster-shop
And sold sweet-meats and ginger-pop.
The small boy then, who owned a cent,
Lacked peace of mind till it was spent,
And shrewd Dame Wilson had an eye
That ogled boys in passing by
And turned their thoughts to cake and pie,
(A tempting bait to such as I.)

The small boy's parent often tried
To switch the tempter off one side
By telling bugbear tales and such
Of "Dame's" contaminating touch,
And said boy's feelings strove to hurt
By hints of eating "pecks of dirt,"
And even going so far to say
In most unappetizing way,
That "Dame" in lieu of daintier stuff,
Nutmegged her custard pies with snuff.
But worse than this we'd have to take,
The boy's abiding faith to shake;
We only knew she served us best
And sent us off supremely blest.
But gone the Wilson's name and fame,
Gone Wilson J. and Wilson Dame;
Fulfilled their humble mission here
As tenants of this mundane sphere.
I see them in my fancy's eye
En-route to mansions in the sky,
Two cheerful cherubs, hand in hand,
With tickets for that better land,
Where it is deemed of slight import ·
If snuff or nutmegs hold the fort.

V.

As added years flew o'er my head,
And added mortals must be fed,
I found my footsteps once more bent
Where squandered I my childish cent.

No more did my experienced eye
Light greedily on cake or pie ;
Necessity must hence prepare
The poor man's meagre bill of fare,
With precious little cake to spare.
I found old Daddy Wilson's space
The people's favorite market place:
Where piped the voice of Wilson J.
In feeble echoes long away,
Now rang the loud stentorian cry
And cheery tones of "Uncle Bi,"
Whose wholesome kindness to the poor,
Should pass him straight through Heaven's door.
Peace to the ashes of a man
Built on a broad and whole-souled plan,
Whose generous heart with courage bold
Was bigger than the ox he sold;
And whose abhorrence of a sham
Brought out an honest Christian "D—n."

VI.

In Eighteen Hundred Sixty One,
And thence until the war was done,
Of all the noted spots in town
Old Knotty Walk is "noted" down ;
(N. B.—weak pun, but spare your frown ;)
In pent up quarters, six by eight,
(Which doth not much exaggerate,)
Would crowds of people congregate

At early morn and often late
To hear the latest news to date
That bore upon the nation's fate.
Here doth my memory revive
A youth exceedingly alive,
Whose dialect was fresh and new
And fairly tinged the ether blue.
Lord! how that youngster used to whoop
Like rooster in a chicken-coop.
O, Charles, as I review you here,
Poetic license, must, I fear,
Appropriate a kindly tear
To blot out much that seems so queer
About thy juvenile career;
In Time's revenges, which are sure,
The law of Average will cure
That which seems crude and immature.
Youth hath its foibles—praised be Heaven
That in the future things may even,
And, like the urchin of our line,
Approximate toward divine.

VII.

Old Knotty Walk, I may not bid
My hand to seal thy coffin-lid
And quite forget the cobbler's den
Which held such pleasure for me then.
Within the building's eastern wing
These merry men would toil and sing,

And hour by hour I heard their jokes
And listened to their hammer-strokes.
Long years ago they passed away,
But visit me a while to-day,
With claim that cannot be denied,
To view the place they occupied.

O shelter for a hundred years
Of human hopes and human fears;
O walls whose echoes rang with glee
In hours of mirth and revelry;
O shadows peering through the gloom
That shrouds each quaint, ghost-haunted room;
From every door and window pane,
I seem to catch a glimpse again
Of some past pilgrim of the town
Who long since laid his burden down.
Good bye, old friends; good bye, old walls;
Ring out the scene; the curtain falls.
I summoned thee with rev'rent hand
From out thy rest in shadow-land;
With sadness more than I may tell
I leave thee with a kind farewell.

The Parson's Ride.

READ AT CHAUTAUQUA CLUB.

I.

This story is one of historic lore,
Of twenty years ago or more;
A story that never was told before;—
Not much of a story as stories go,
But the point of which, as you easily know,
Depends on whether the actual facts
Make up for the merit the telling lacks;
And the story I tell, or the song that I sing,
(Whatever you style the rendering)
Is not a feather from Fancy's wing,
Or a long drawn bow on Fiction's string,
But a regular bona-fide thing,
Wherein in a sorrowful role did shine
A respected clerical friend of mine.
Now, this friend was not an adventurous man,
Built on a harum-scarum plan;
It wasn't a part of his gospel creed
To indulge in fun that he did not need,
Or secular things to unduly heed;

A novel he seldom cared to read,
And of wine and cigars used little indeed,
Nor were his finances made to bleed -
In betting on the rate of speed
That might be wrung from the winning steed.
His opinion of cards we never knew,
But we don't believe that he ever drew
    A fraudulent Jack
    From the back of the pack,
To play a trick on me or you ;
And dancing? Well, he may have done it,
But only as women choose a bonnet—
For Fashion's sake—and not because
Of anything founded on Reason's laws.
But to sum him up in an off-hand way,
He cared for work much more than play,
Which is quite in advance of what you can say,
Of most of the fellows we meet to-day ;
This fairly represents the chap
That forms the subject of our mishap.

II.

From Westville Hamlet to Taunton Green
Is as straight a way as ever was seen,
With only a couple of miles between,
And an easy path to follow I ween,
And even a minister's spavined beast
Should make the trip in an hour at least.

But on one weird and stormy night,
When the moon and stars were hid from sight;
When darkness was naught but a solid abyss,
And Egypt was sunlight, compared to this,
Our friend hitched up his ancient plug,
By the glow of a transient lightning bug,
And made a trip which in merited fame
Should immortalize the rider's name.

III.

But why this drive that fateful hour,
In face of such a drenching shower
    As would make old Noah
    In jealousy roar,
Because he plied his ancient oar
So many centuries before,
And lost his chance to tie this score?
There's a saying somewhere down in the books
By one of your cynical bachelor crooks,
That in every case of trouble and bother,
A woman is tied at one end or the other;
    Of course your bard
    Doesn't speak by the card,
His lot not being uncommonly hard;
But we find it an easy affair to trace
The woman who shone in the parson's case
And started him off on a wild goose chase.
    For it came to pass,
    That a certain lass,
Who wished to attend a Chautauqua class,

Pre-empted a seat by the Parson's side
And shared his lot on this evening ride.

IV.

And now farewell while we take our leave,
With never a thought there was cause to grieve,
As away they go on that stormy eve,
For who would ever dare to believe
What a web of woe that ride could weave.
And as Oliver Wendell, whose name was Holmes,
Remarks with feeling in one of his "pomes":
    "We'll surrender their forms
    To the God of the storms,
    The lightning and gale,"
    The snow, rain and hail,
And all that's attached to the weather detail;
For if sparrows are kindly shown the way,
Why, preachers, of course, should fare better than they.
Once more farewell as away they go,
On a journey so eternally slow
That before they reached the town below
His fair companion's cup of woe
Would fill to the brim and overflow,
Because her cake was mostly dough.

V.

From the start to the finish the record is lost,
The parson not deeming it worth the cost.

And from all you have ever heard him say,
He has quite forgotten that trying day.
But we have learned that late that night,
A clerical-got-up sort of wight
Was found in the sorriest kind of a plight
On the track of the county cattle-show site.
    No mortal below
    Will ever know
How many times about that track
His steed had been obliged to tack,
Or gather from the sorry jade
A record of the time she made.
Of course no one would ever dare
To hint that the minister wanted to swear,
Yet we reckon that many a Bible word,
With more than usual emphasis stirred,
On the cattle-show ground that night was heard,
And that never before rang out so strong
The cry—"How long, O Lord, how long!"

VI.

    Ah! Parson Blank,
    You'll little thank
Your humble servant, the rhyming crank,
For spreading abroad to the world outside
The painful facts of that evening ride,
Yet we all are rapped by Fate at times,
And even the fellow that made the rhymes

Remembers his little escapade
Which he wouldn't for worlds have dragged on parade.
It certainly could not be charged to you
That the road that night ran all askew,
And a turnpike way as straight as a line
From a couple of miles stretched out to nine.
I know there were some who wickedly said
The Chautauqua student muddled your head,
But this was only gossiping chat,
And of course we couldn't take stock in that;
And other ones asked in peculiar tone:
"Does he always let whiskey and such alone?"
But those were fellows who couldn't be just,
Who never take any person on trust,
Who make it a practice to go on a bust,
And so they believe that a parson must.
Oh! no, you can't make us believe
That liquor, or any daughter of Eve
Could lead his head so far astray
As to make him give himself away,
But rather one of those curious haps
That Providence sets as human traps,—
Which mortal man has labored in vain
On logical grounds to clearly explain;
To some such scapegoat we ascribe
Hard luck and all its kindred tribe.

* * * * * * * *

Long years ago this verse was spun
And carelessly woven in frolicsome fun,

But alack! for the ravage of ruthless Time
A soberer vein creeps into my rhyme;
Our friend the parson is laid at rest
With the honest souls who have lived their best,
And I doff my jest in a reverent mood
To the ashes of one so true and good.
May his kindly spirit know no pain
As we take the humorous ride again,
And his memory be no less revered
By the hearts that the pleasant lines have cheered.
I somehow fancy that we may be loved
The more for the joy that our mirth has moved,
And I sing my song in the fullest belief
That its measure brings our friend no grief.

MORAL.

All men may come to grief; the path of life
Is full of darkest ways and stumbling blocks;
Even in safest poise our lot is rife
With danger from rude, unexpected knocks.
The preacher and the layman share alike
In all the common hardships of the race,
And fate is quite as prone to roughly strike
The saint as soon as sinner in the face.
This lesson we might teach; take heed
On every journey that you undertake;
Not to rely too heavily on speed,
Which does not always reach the winning stake.
A moderate slowness may seem somewhat tame,
But probably you'll get there all the same.

BLACK JACK.

A MEMORY OF WEIR STREET.

Way back in the days of my juvenile past,
There were pictures of childhood whose colors were fast;
    And the years that have sped
    O'er my thinly clad head
Only show how our early impressions will last.
'Twas a curious burgh—this old township of ours,
Filled with legends that idleness fondly devours,
And in stirring the embers of memory's host,
I have raked from the ashes full many a ghost.
In a little, old shanty not far down the street,
On a site where convivial spirits now meet;
    (And to better locate,
    Let the writer here state—
Strike a line from Main street, keep an eye to the left,
Till you come to a shop of its tenants bereft,
Round the corner of which the curious eye
A phenomenal vine of the grape may espy.)
    Just about on that spot
    Did we small boys pay "scot"
To a "darkey" who dealt in cake, candy and pie.

Now this quizzical gent of an ebony hue
Was a curious sample of human to view,
    With a hump on his back,
    And most gloomily black,
Well known the town over as ancient Black Jack.
There was much in his feature and more in his shape
That suggested a brotherly kin to the ape.
    I can see the old "coon"
    On a warm afternoon,—
One of nature's inharmonies shorn of all tune,
    Half asleep, half awake,
    With an eye to his cake,
And extremely alive to a chance on the make.
    Of his age no man knew,
    But if half told were true
He had lived the most part of a century through.
Indeed, there were those who enlarged on the truth,
And facetiously claimed that the date of his youth
Required a "B. C." and boldly declared
That Jack was an infant that Herod had spared.
    But we can't be exact
    With regard to each fact,
As history often gets fearfully whacked.
    Yet suffice it to say
    That there lingers to-day
In the minds of old stagers a luminous ray
Of remembrance concerning this person of shade,
Who was known as Black Jack—more correctly, John
    Slade;

And I fancy when travelling through Weir street some
　　night,
'Mid the spectre-like shadows that form in the light,
　　That perhaps I shall meet
　　　　Poor old Jack on the street,
And gather the news from his latest retreat;
For that Jack had a soul never harbor a doubt,
And that Jack owns a ghost that can ramble about,
Is as certain as any or all of the facts
That are borne out by Testament, pulpit or tracts.
'Twas a dreary existence he led upon earth,
Minus all that can make one's existence of worth;
Small knowledge he had of the why and the whence
Of his being, and knowing much less of the hence.
Grant his spirit a chance in the ages to come
To haunt the grim shades of his whilom old home,
　　Where are spirits to-day
　　That are blocking the way,
Less divine than the soul that enlivened Jack's clay.
　　And the Lord has made thin
　　　　The color of skin,
So it's fair to presume that He'll summon Jack in.
　　Here's kind thought for Black Jack,
　　　　With no pack on his back
To hamper his race on the heavenly track;
　　And here's hoping that we
　　　　May find record as free
From the follies and vices of life as did he.

UNCLE JIM.

Drives the coachman through the streets,
    All the day;
Greeting every one he meets
    On the way.
Forty years or more has seen
Him going through the same routine,—
Driving to and from the Green,
    So they say.

Truer knight of rein and whip,
    Hard to find;
Never with a saucy lip
    Seems inclined;
Kind to all the boys as well,
As you never hear them tell
That he notices the yell—
    "Whip behind."

Many rides he's given free
    To the poor;
Greater saint than you or me,
    I am sure.
But it grieves us to rehearse,—
Often helped the lame in purse,
Who took no pains to reimburse,
    Evermore.

Philosophic kind of man—
    Uncle James,

Though he mayn't approve our plan—
  Calling names.
Every day is peaceful spent;
Though he hasn't made a cent,
Yet he's just as well content,
  So he claims.

When or why he struck the town,
  No one knows;
Roads were bad and fares were down,
  I suppose;
Though this jovial knight of reins
In his merry mood maintains
That the roads are always "lanes"
  Where he goes.

Blest be cheery Uncle Jim
  All his days;
Would that we were more like him —
  Many ways;
Would that Fortune might send down
On our bald and shining crown,
As on his, no shadowy frown,—
  Only praise.

When he climbs the "Golden Stair"
  Some bright day,
He'll not have to drop a fare
  Or to pay;
Gabriel's voice will reach his ear—
"He whose record shines so clear,
Needs to show no tickets here;"
  "Step this way."

(Uncle Jim" has since climbed the Golden Stairs, and there is no doubt but that he occupies a reserved seat.)

AT MOUNT PLEASANT.

(A REVERIE.)

I stand within the city of the dead;
  I need but idly cast my eyes around
To note the spot where many a grassy mound
  Has given shelter to some weary form
  Who, from the beatings of Life's cruel storm,
Has pillowed here in sleep his weary head;
Has ceased to struggle with his hopes and fears;
  Has fought his battle bravely to the last;
And, save the homage of a few brief tears,
  Left to a sadly-soon forgotten past.
And here, where earthly bonds relax their power,
  And human passions shall no more be stirred;
Where, in the quiet of an evening hour,
  Almost a whisper's echo might be heard,
And seems an easy task for mortal hand
To touch the borders of another land;—
So fair this spot, and yet, alas! so drear,
A weird enchantment ever lingering near,
Inviting rest in such a dubious voice,
One well might shudder e'er he makes the choice;

Here may we come for thought; the soul of man
    Would scarcely dare this sacred place profane
With grosser life; with petty scheme and plan
    That drag existence to its lowest plane.

And on the marble's face I read of one
    Almost forgotten with the lapse of years,
Who shared in earlier days my boyish fun
    And mingled with my own his grief and tears;
And I am thinking—had my friend been spared
To tread the path of active life till now,
What lofty purposes he might have dared—
    What well-earned laurels placed upon his brow.
Ah! friend, companion, we may never know
    How much of life was buried in thy grave;
    How much of what was noble, true and brave
Has never come to fruitage here below;
But we may build an ideal in our thought,
    So richly happy in the "might have been,"
That all reality should sink to naught
    Beside the visions of the fair unseen:
And we may thank kind Providence for this—
    Perhaps the greatest boon that mortals know,
That his might be to taste of human bliss,
    But not to drain the dregs of human woe.
Sleep on, dear friend, in blissfulness of peace;
The sorrows of the living never cease,
And all these years in peaceful slumber spent,
Have marked a restful season of content.

Man of the world, whose tireless, busy life
Has made existence little but a strife;

Who only sees within Earth's fair domain,
An endless battle-ground for sordid gain,
'Twere well at times you should a moment spare
And drop this everlasting round of care;
Is is not worth your while an hour to give
To better learn for what and whom you live?
To share the good with which your lot is blessed,
With those a harsher fate has sore oppressed?
For you and I must come to this some day;
   Some day will lie neglected and alone,
   Beneath the shadow of a soulless stone
That has but empty compliments to pay;
That speaks in mocking tones in stranger's ears,
   A tale of virtues that we ne'er possessed,
While friends who knew our weakness drop their tears
   To plead for faults of which we stood confessed.
Through all the ages years shall come and go;
The tides of life resistless ebb and flow,
And day by day an unrelenting hand
Shall lead new comers to the shadow land.
Like these, they too shall sleep a dreamless sleep,
While sun and moon and stars their vigils keep
To guard in all that's beautiful and best,
The endless slumbers of a world of rest.

RHYMES;

PHILOSOPHIC AND PERSONAL.

1—A Pulpit 'Echo.
2—Blifkins.
3—Reflections from Thanatopsis.
4—Not Unhappy.
5—Acrostical.
6—My Neighbor and I.
7—Speculation in Futures.
8—Salad for the Conceited.
9—Review of the Old School-boys.
10—A Spasm of Charity.
11—Not so Old as he Thinks.
12—Skeesick—a Domestic Idyl.
13—May, 1882—Real and Ideal.
14—School Day Memories.
15—Polo.
16—My Rhymes.

A Pulpit Echo.

"Day unto day uttereth speech, and night unto night showeth knowledge."

I.

Day unto day I scrub along,—
One of a weary, worrying throng,
The burden of whose speech and song—
    A cry for bread and butter;
Night unto night I vainly seek
That knowledge of which prophets speak—
And find it answered all too weak—
    This cry I daily utter.

II.

Day unto day I build anew
Some scheme to pull "your uncle" through,
And change his mood to pink from blue,
    Thus making life seem brighter;
Night unto night I grasp my broom,
When "all to smash" has gone my boom,
And sweep the ruins from my room,—
    A wiser, sadder fighter.

III.

Day unto day some heartless chap,
Who rates my feelings not a "rap,"
Will give a most uncalled-for slap
   Where I have grown most tender.
Night unto night I lie awake
A most un-Christian plan to make
To duplicate that chap's mistake,
   And sin with greater splendor.

IV.

Day unto day a "still, small voice"
Will make a fellow's heart rejoice,
By giving him a half-way choice
   'Twixt what is good and evil.
Night unto night when worn with fight
In dodging wrong and hunting right,
Lo and behold, bobs up in sight
   Our ancient friend, the Devil.

V.

Day unto day I look around
And see some tempted mortal found
On what is styled "forbidden ground"
   By those whose luck was greater.
Night unto night I think up strong
This theory of right and wrong,
Thankful the deal does not belong
   To me, but the Creator.

VI.

Day unto day, I can't tell why,
  (Perhaps you know as well as I,)
I look to see the clouds roll by
    And clear up Life's horizon.
Night unto night the sun will set
  (At least it never failed as yet,)
And leave me in the same old fret—
    A state of mental "pison."

VII.

Yes, speech is heard "day unto day,"
Exactly as the Scriptures say,
And loud the preachers preach and pray;
    But, zealous Christian brother—
Night unto night has made us think
(So hard we couldn't sleep a wink)
That half the speech was wasted ink,
    And fruitless talk the other.

VIII.

Day unto day, if we are wise,
And look around with kinder eyes,
We'll find much less to criticise
    In those we see about us.
Night unto night in seeking rest,
I'm growing more and more impressed
That, even at our very best,
    The world can do without us.

BLIFKINS.

A TALE OF ORPHANAGE

Upon the window sill I spy
   An orphan lorn and lone;
There's melancholy in his eye,
   And sadness in his tone.

Deserted by maternal care,
   And left unto the fates,
He seeks his gastronomic fare,
   From cold and empty plates.

What soothes poor Blifkins in this hour
   Of orphaned solitude,
Unless through some kind, ruling power
   He finds his hopes renewed?

The widow and the orphan long
   Have read of friends in need,
Such hopes to Blifkins scarce belong,
   For Blifkins can not read.

"Like as a father pitieth child"—
   Such is the way it's put,
But Blifkins' father runneth wild
   With unparental foot.

O, hard and harsh humanity,—
    By cruel passions torn,
That heedeth not the orphan's-cry,
    Though countless Blifkins mourn.

If thou couldst look that saddened phiz
    Of Blifkins in the face,
And view his sorrow as it is,
    It might enhance your grace.

So many hearts are tightly locked,
    And hid secure the key,
That though a thousand Blifkins knocked,
    They'd scarce the keyhole see.

And I am wasting precious ink
    For what must come to naught,
While Blifkins nothing does but blink,
    In answer to my thought.

But weep not, friend, nor waste wild grief,
    In passing round your hat,
This case will scarce admit relief,
    For Blifkins is a cat.

REFLECTIONS FROM THANATOPSIS.

AN ENDORSEMENT OF WM. CULLEN BRYANT.

"The gay will laugh when thou art gone,"
    Says Wm. Cullen;
Prophetic singer, "right you be;"
This world will have its jamboree
When you and I are trod upon
    Beneath the Mullein.

Momus will hold his festive court,
    Though we are minus,
And merry hearts with jocund glee
Will little reck of you or me,
While those who stay and hold the fort,
    Not long enshrine us.

"The solemn brood of care plod on,"
    Observes friend Bryant;
Nature pursueth, grave or gay,
The even tenor of her way;
'Tis man alone who cannot don
    An air defiant.

"And each one as before, will chase
    His favorite phantom;"
Alas! for all thy lofty pride,
Thou with conceit intensified;
Thou only struttest in thy place,—
    A feeble bantam.

Inflated souls with pride immense,
    Hold the idea,
That when they cease their mortal clack,
The world will go to Ballyhack,
But whence they draw such inference,
    Is not so clear.

In point of fact, note the reverse;—
    In all such cases,
Some other fellows will be found
Whose shoes will cover far more ground,
And better men, instead of worse,
    Will take their places.

An hour of sorrow and of grief
    Attends our exit,
And healing Time slips in and shares
Its newer joys and fresher cares,
Which tend to give the heart relief
    And not perplex it.

But Bryant seems to hold the key
    To the position—
  "So live that when thy summons comes,
  Go not like slaves," tied by the thumbs,
As though the journey were to be
    Straight to perdition.

But let the record of thy years
    Shine out so brightly,
  That there can linger no mistrust
  Of aught malignant or unjust,
Nor shall the sad reproach of tears
    Chide e'er so lightly.

Then laugh, ye gay, and dance and sing
    Though years bring sorrow;
  Let men and women come and go
  And chase their phantoms to and fro;
What matters it if Time shall bring
    A glad to-morrow?

NOT UNHAPPY.

I meet a friend upon my daily walk:
   One of the rare, uplifted sort of chaps,
   Who rise above the pitiful mishaps
At which so many of us turn and balk:
And this my constant greeting as we meet—
   "Friend, are you happy?" With contented smile,
   As he were half an angel all the while,
And needed only wings to be complete,
"I'm not unhappy"—thus he makes reply
With calm assurance that I may not doubt,
And I am sent away to wonder why
   My friend should learn a trick I've not found out.
"Not quite unhappy?" Confident and strong,
This ever is the burden of his song.

And yet beyond all doubt my friend has learned
   One of the truest lessons of the hour,—
   That sweet contentment in its restful power
Is not an acquisition to be spurned.
We would be happy—idiots that we are,
   Striving, with hurrying feet and longing eyes,
   For glimpses of that weak fool's Paradise,
Which tells of pleasure with no shade of care.
Be not unhappy, and thy lot is cast
   For all the joy that falleth to thy share,
Nor grief nor trouble, howe'er deep or vast,
   Shall bring more burdens than thy soul can bear.
Yes, friend, you're doubtless right; yet, none the less,
But few of us attain to happiness.

ACROSTICAL.

TO MY FRIEND.

C ould all the friendships of our life on earth,
H ave the rare value of your honest worth,
A iming to act with conscience ever clear,
R ejecting all that makes life insincere,
L avish in every generous deed and thought,
E steeming only acts where good is wrought,
S o rich in all the traits to virtue kin,

E nnobling through their power to charm and win;
D earer such friendships than the flimsy ties,
W hich in their way, speak but so many lies,
A nd when ill-fortune threatens to control,
R eveal their wretched poverty of soul.
D oubtful of such, we, hoping to be just,

P rize more the blessing of a generous trust,
R ich in its honest thought and simple ways
A nd all unconscious of deserving praise.—
T his is the gift in every age and place
T hat brings the greatest blessing to the race.

My Neighbor and I.

I have a neighbor prone to fret
And fall into a needless sweat,
Belittling his life and soul,
Because of things he can't control.
I, by good luck, was early taught
That fretting mostly came to naught,
Or, if some life it introduced,
Bred curses that came home to roost.

My neighbor has been blessed in store;
Blessed, did I say? Nay, cursed the more,
Since all his stores of worldly pelf
Have brought no blessing to himself.
Much happier I in mild content,
With but the little Fate has sent,
And deem myself not much the worse
Because I hold an empty purse.

My neighbor grumbles at the rain
Because it breeds rheumatic pain;
He also frowns on sunny days
And growls at Phœbus' scorching rays.

I see no reason to complain
Either of sunshine or of rain,
And am convinced beyond a doubt
That neither should be counted out.

My neighbor is a haughty man,
Built on a high and mighty plan,
Who summons men with beck and nod
As if he were a demi-god.
I take no stock in pride of caste,
Which surely comes to grief at last,
And entertain my private whim
That parti-walls of such are slim.

My neighbor pays but little heed
To suffering mortals in their need;
His dollars have that curious chink
Which stops his power to hear or think.
I find I get a dividend
In playing sympathetic friend,
And half the fun of life is lost,
If offered to us free of cost.

And now perhaps I've made you see
The difference 'twixt him and me,
He could not be me if he would;
I would not be him if I could.
It may be best that we should move
Each in his individual groove,
Yet there's a difference I opine,
Between my neighbor's lot and mine.

Speculation in Futures.

Sooner or later Life's weak flickering flame
    Grows dim and ceases;
Sooner or later this poor human frame
    Will go to pieces.

Sooner or later shall we feel the touch
    Of frosty fingers;
Sooner or later shall we know how much
    Our memory lingers.

Sooner or late our mourners will begin
    Their doubtful grievings;
Sooner or late will creditors step in
    And take the leavings.

Sooner or late will gossip have its fun
    Bred from the scandal
That, sure as direst fate pours out when one
    Goes off the handle.

Sooner or later we must all endure
    Posthumous chinning:—
Those compliments that come too late to cure
    Us of our sinning.

"A small-souled chap he was,"—some one will say,
    "Cut for a low fit;"
"The probabilities are strong to-day
    He's safe in Tophet."

Another, kind of heart, will criticise
    Us less severely,
Looking at what were sins in other eyes,
    As errors merely.

Ah! me, what will it matter to us then—
    The world's opinion?
We'll fly our banners and our fortunes in
    A new dominion.

But when that time shall come to you and me,
    Sooner or later,
Thank Heaven, no Mrs. Grundy then will be
    Our arbitrator.

And as the "ins" and "outs" are figured up,
    And told our story,
Who knows but even we may have a sup
    And taste of glory?

And though we may unwisely have betrayed
    Erratic fancies,
Let's hope that some allowance may be made
    For circumstances.

Let's hope, that though our judge we've sorely tried,
    Some little item
May find a place upon our credit side
    And quite delight him.

Sooner or later will the business end,
    The plot unravel;
Sooner or later, my respected friend,
    We'll have to travel.

SALAD FOR THE CONCEITED.

Of all conceits that haunt a man
    And hedge themselves about him,
There never was one since Time began,
That seemed so poor and thin to scan,
As the thought that the world was built on a plan,
    That it couldn't get on without him.

A conceit as old as the world is this,
    And quite correct in Adam,
For it wouldn't be strange that Eve might miss
The only man who could give the kiss
Which settled the fact of connubial bliss
    Between himself and madam.

But times have changed, we are forced to believe,
    And Adams are getting more plenty;
And the chances to-day that a modern Eve
Would go far out of her way to grieve,
Should her lord and master take his leave,
    Would scarcely be one in twenty.

And though you may deem the reasons rife,
    For keeping in recollection,
'Tis not alone the comforted wife
Who drives your memory out of her life,
But oblivion's many-bladed knife
    Will cut in every direction.

And, friend, should you entertain a whim
   That your loss the world might cripple,
We grieve your pride of heart to dim,
But the place you fill is so very slim,
You might go under and cease to swim,
   Without creating a ripple.

Now out of this a "conundrum" springs—
   Wherefore this fuss and labor,
This working so hard for material things,
That are more than likely to take on wings,
When possession no more happiness brings
   To you than your poorer neighbor?

We give it up and pass it along,
   As have they who lived before us;
We try, as did they, to come out strong,
But things sometimes go fearfully wrong,
And we all of us sing the same old song
   With but little change in the chorus.

May not this folly of human conceit
   Be a part of the plan eternal—
That a man should struggle with weary feet,
In weak endeavors to win a heat
Of a race which shall never be complete,
   Till we reach the goal supernal?

Then sound your trumpet and blow your horn
   And make the most of your merits;
There's many a man who contrives to adorn
A position for which he never was born,
And the world has nothing for him but scorn,
   Who's content with what he inherits.

Review of the Old School Boys.

"So these were boys;"—these with the care-worn look
   Of two-score years or more upon their brow;
Were these grim fellows we are greeting now,
The old-time urchins of the slate and book?
He with the sober phiz and trim cravat—
   Whose face scarce ever breaks into a smile;
Was this the youth who donned the old straw hat
   And barefoot trudged for many a weary mile?

And this strong burly chap of fourteen stone,
   Who romped in boyish sport upon the Green;
In those old days didst ever think, I ween,
That thine would be the saddest task of all,—
To shroud and decorate the funeral pall
Of friends and schoolmates thou so well hast known?

And one whose name appeared upon the list,
   Who wandered from us at an early day;—
I wonder if the little boy we missed,
   Has laid his youthful looks and pranks away;
I think of him with fresh and ruddy cheek—
   This truant bee from our scholastic hive,
I have in mind a child with bearing meek,
   And not the bearded man of forty-five.

And thou, whose genial look and pleasant eye
  Foreshadowed even in that youthful time,
    The proud fulfilment of thy manhood's prime ;
Did'st ever once a thought possess thy brain,
That thou wouldst play the soldier o'er again
With deadly arms and earnest battle cry?
Didst ever think that on some hard-fought field,
Where either combatant disdained to yield,
That thou wouldst bear away the cruel scar
That marks the terrors of "grim-visaged war"?
Ah! dear old comrades, we but little thought
The mimic battles that we daily fought,
Were embryotic forms of real strife,
To paint the conflicts of a struggling life.
How little did our boyish reasoning mark
  The ebb and flow of all those troub'lous tides,
Whose narrow channels are but treacherous guides
Upon the stream where human lives embark:
And yet the boy is father to the man ;
  And did we know it, each of us might trace
Even in childhood, the imperfect plan
  That in the years must stare us in the face.
Alas! we learn the lesson all too late
To shape for wisest ends our earthly fate.
One thing alone is taught us hard and fast—
We are but boys, and shall be to the last.

A SPASM OF CHARITY.

A friendless lad stood on the street,
As poor a boy as you could meet,
Shrunken in form and bare of feet,
Arrayed in garb quite incomplete,
And looking anything but neat.

One of the poorest of God's poor:—
A little waif on Life's bleak moor,
Begging his bread from door to door;
Through all his years of nothing sure
Except to suffer and endure.

Now this poor boy so meanly clad
Would not have seemed to be a lad
To wake one's interest, good or bad,
And yet a thought akin to sad,
Aroused what sympathy I had.

A thought like this ran through my mind—
Suppose the Fates had been inclined
To fix my lot in human kind
Like this poor lad's, so dark and blind,
That I must ever grope behind.

And yet it's but a game of chance,
Whether in Life we weep or dance,
So much may some light circumstance,
(It may be but a friendly glance,)
Our earthly happiness enhance.

And feeling thus I did not dare
To pass the boy who lingered there
With look forlorn and form half bare,
Without a small attempt to share
The little that I had to spare.

Ye mortals of a selfish clan,
Rest easy if you easy can,
But surely it was Heaven's plan
That charity should be the span
To bridge 'twixt man and fellow-man.

NOT SO OLD AS HE THINKS.

Grim shades of Methuselah, dead and grown cold,
Who might this chap be that assumes we are old?
Perhaps the old croaker would speak for himself,
But we're not prepared to be laid on the shelf.

Would he have you suppose we are knocked out of time?
Why bless his dear soul we are just in our prime,
And we answer the roll-call at morn, noon and eve,
With a promptness that makes our dear landlady grieve.

Does the fellow imagine he's telling the truth
When he says we have outlived the days of our youth?
Can't he learn it—or must he forever be told—
"There's a class of good people that never grow old?"

Does he think it because we can't dance like a top,
Or wear the nonsensical airs of a fop?
Does he reckon a touch of incipient gout
As a sign that your uncle is nearly played out?

Does he get his queer notions concerning our years
From the baldness of occiput over the ears,
When it long since was settled beyond any doubt,
That a surplus of brainage must make its way out?

Because he has found in our phiz a new crease,
Does he think we've let up on Mortality's lease?
Can't he learn that a wrinkle may be but a sign
Of a vein in a large intellectual mine?

Can't the blunderbuss see that a few silvered hairs
Mark the progress less often of years than of cares,
While a man may be many removes from the dead
And yet bloom like a snowball all over his head?

But, perhaps after all, it may chance that he's right,
For Time steals a march like a thief in the night,
And we find the boy soldier in youthfulness fair,
Enrolled as a veteran e'er he's aware.

Ah! the days of our youth all too soon slip away,
And Life is so brief to the happy and gay,
That it startles our senses to hear the grim call
That sooner or later must come to us all.

But we build up our lives more on hopes than on fears,
While the heart may keep young in the fullness of years
So the friends who best know us need not to be told
Why we see no good reason for feeling so old.

"SKEESICK."

A DOMESTIC IDYL.

We carol forth our rhythmic measures
In adulation of the treasures
   That make our earthly life a blessing;—
Our household gods; our worldly pelf;
Our—last, but not the least—ourself;
   Each some poetic worth possessing.

"Our household gods," not always human,
Assuming shape of man or woman,
   Are those whose lives have circled round us;
But quite unlike in form or feature,
Perhaps a dumb and soulless creature
   With almost human ties has bound us.

And, as my evening chair I sit in
And gaze upon our last year's kitten
   Now grown to be a staid grimalkin,
Whose muse (mews) like mine, I sadly fear,
Shall grow more torturing to the ear
   As more and more it fills the welkin.

My thoughts are kindling to a fancy,
That I would, by some necromancy,
   Just play at pussy in the corner,
And look on life as fun and frolic,
Untainted with the melancholic
   That placards every man a mourner.

I wonder does his dreamy winking—
That curious mode of feline blinking,
   Betoken an inborn contentment,
Or whether after human fashions,
He feels those despicable passions
   That we call hatred and resentment.

But signs of back and tail uprising,
Would indicate it not surprising
   If he his name had heard us mention,
Though by what law of metaphysics,
A cat should bear the name of Skeesicks,
   Is quite beyond my comprehension.

Ah! kit that was, old cat that now is,
The record of your martial prowess
   Disturbs us in our midnight slumbers,
And trumpet-tongued, nocturnal yelling,
Your feats of arms, (and claws) are telling,
   More eloquent than poet's numbers.

And after all it little matters—
The form of life that fortune scatters,—
   The class or order, name or station,
A cat may look upon his highness;"
The king shall match the cat for slyness,
   Both parts of one complete creation.

MAY, 1882.

THE IDEAL—WRITTEN MAY 1st.

A welcome to the gladsome month of May,
 With sunny smiles and sweetly fragrant flowers,
 As once adorned the legendary bowers
In fairy pictures of our childhood's day.
Welcome, the glories of this queen of Spring,
Whose sights and sounds give pledges, heralding
Throughout her realms, a more than regal reign
Of tropic splendor crowned with golden gain.
Last of the vernal months, we love her best;
 Upon the threshold of a winter past,
She shuts the door and promises sweet rest
 From angry storm and from the chilling blast.
The smiles upon her face are wondrous fair,
And Heaven's own incense floats upon the air.

THE REAL—WRITTEN MAY 31st.

A plague upon the wretched month of May,
 With doleful frowns and drizzling, wilting showers
 As once beguiled traditionary hours
In Bible stories of old Noah's day;
Banish the mem'ries of this blight of Spring,
Whose sights and sounds gave pledges, heralding
Throughout her realms, a more than needful rain
Of fearful wetness and of muddy pain.
Last of the vernal months, she's done her best;
 Upon the threshold of a winter past
She holds the door ajar, and for the rest,
 See "Weather Probs," with every day o'ercast.
The smiles upon her face are all askew,
And Heaven's own incense but a heavy dew.

SCHOOL DAY MEMORIES.

A RESPONSE.

Ah! no, my friend, you would not know
    That lakeside wood to-day;
The joys and charms of long ago
    Are spirited away.

The demon of a restless change
    Has exercised its spell
And shadowed magic-like and strange,
    The haunts you loved so well.

No longer in a little lane
    Do sun and shadow meet;
The rustic path across the plain
    Is now a spacious street.

The fragrance of the summer air
    Is banished from the spot;
Those melodies so sweet and rare,
    To-day, alas, are not.

The music of the gentle brook,
    The song of birds and bees,
The rustic chair in cosy nook,
    The murm'ring of the breeze,

These all are pleasures of a past
    That will not reappear;—
Phantoms of joys that could not last
    Beyond our childhood's year.

And he whose whisper brought a blush
    Into a cheek that day,
Is lying in the churchyard hush
    Beneath a slab of gray.

Our school-days live but as a dream
    Of idle play and sport,
And Youth as a poetic theme
    With Fancy holding court.

Oh! no, my friend, 'tis not the same;
    A Force of mighty power
Is working, with mysterious aim,
    A change with every hour.

Be this the joy that ever springs
    From memory's smiles or tears;—
They lead to higher, better things
    Through all the coming years.

POLO.

AS SEEN BY THE LOCAL PHILOSOPHER.

We'd like first-rate, if we had time,
Old Mount Parnassus' heights to climb,
And wrestle at a little rhyme
    On what we saw at Polo.

The game that rolls on every tongue,
Of which the ancients never sung,—
A game of "go it while you're young,"—
    This wondrous game of Polo.

Where wisest heads and craziest cranks
Alike combine to swell the ranks
Who crowd to watch the sportive pranks
    That animate the Polo.

Where maidens fair and stately dame
Are fascinated with the game,
And even cripples, halt and lame
    Will hobble to the Polo.

Where, sandwiched in with boys and men,
Are patriarchs—"fourscore and ten,"
And infants born—we won't say when;
    But old enough for Polo.

And chaps were there in motley dress.
With half a garment on—or less,
Like human signals of distress,
   Set for a game of Polo.

A game of doubtful "outs" and "ins,"
Where muscle more than science wins,
And broken heads and blackened shins
   Are trophies of the Polo.

And thus I wondered as I gazed,—
Why all this rumpus should be raised,
And half the city should be crazed
   About a game of Polo.

And men and women nightly flock
And wait from seven till ten o'clock
To see a lot of fellows knock
   A ball about at Polo.

Yet, criticise it as you will,
The world will ride its hobbies still;
And so, if Polo fills the bill,
   Why take it out in Polo.

My Rhymes

Are but the children of an idle hour;
Weak intellectual buds, forced into flower;
Thought-bubbles, surface-rising, that contain
The lighter products of a busy brain.
Born of a sudden whim or passing thought,
With more of art than inspiration fraught,
I tire of constant toil and care at times
And find companionship in simple rhymes.
As a rude player wandering o'er the keys,
Can scarce expect a cultured ear to please,
Yet by some chance may touch upon a strain
That echoes with a glad and sweet refrain,
So I, though striving simply to rehearse
For self-enjoyment, my too feeble verse,
Have, all unconscious, chanted many a tone
That touched a heart responsive to my own,
Awakening in another's weary lot,
Some grain of comfort he had nigh forgot,
And homeward circling to its native air,
Breathed a new friendship ere I was aware:
And though we never clasped each others hands,
But dwell as denizens of foreign lands,
Yet through a strangely kind, benignant law,
It chances that a face I never saw,

In warmest sympathy and love may shine,
Beaming with hope at some stray thought of mine.

And so I build and launch the little boat
That sets a measure of my song afloat,
And watch the voyage with a quiet sport,
Contented though it never reach a port.
It was my venture; though to other eyes
The cargo might seem neither rich nor wise;
What matters it though all the world condemn?
To me each one contained some little gem;
I know they are not diamonds; but the poor
Can hardly hope to own a Koh-i-nor.
The merest pennies in the beggar's clutch
Outweigh the guinea in the rich man's touch:
Call mine the beggar's pennies if you will;
What care I, if my humble need they fill?
Coined from the heart, no spurious sound they ring,
Like the charmed voices with which sirens sing.
More of God's offspring feed on crumbs than cake,
And lightest wine the keenest thirst may slake;
Then who shall say but that my halting line
May reach and cheer another heart than mine,
While the poor nonsense of a lighter mood
May have its helpful influence for good,
Teaching a lesson in its weak, crude way,
That otherwise I had no power to say.
May not my feeble plea in part excuse
The vagaries that haunt my wandering muse,
And kindly hearts fresh confidence shall bring
To lift the measure of the songs I sing.

SERMONETTES.

1—THE GOOD SAMARITAN.
2—THE PARSON'S STORY.
3—MORE BLESSED TO GIVE THAN TO RECEIVE.
4—AN OLD STORY REVISED.
5—DONE ON BOTH SIDES.
6—A QUERY.
7—GOOSE EGG HATCHED OUT.

THE GOOD SAMARITAN.

  There's an old allegorical,
  Biblo-historical
Tale, (a conundrum it proved in its time,)
  Called "Who is my neighbor?"
  And if not too much labor,
Suppose we rehearse it and set it to rhyme.

A Jerusalem-ite had started down
To visit his uncle in Jericho town;
And in stating the facts the writer grieves
To say that the traveler fell among thieves,
Who got in their work in that damaging way
So characteristic of thieves to this day;
For not content with rifling his purse,
(Which to fellows like us, there could nothing be worse,)
  They showed him no mercy
  But quite "vice-versa,"
They cut up and "raised most particular Ned,"
By stripping and leaving the fellow half dead.

Now the first individual passing that way,
Was a man of devout ministerial way,

Who prayed every hour with an unctuous zest,
That the Lord would be kind to the sick and oppressed,
    And of course you would think,
    As quick as a wink,
That this virtuous man would be victuals and drink,
    But we're sorry to state
    That that hook did'nt bait,
And he left the poor Jew all alone to his fate;
    For the narrative goes
    That he followed his nose
And closed his eyes to the victim's woes.

Now who is this fellow that struts in the van?
Ah! here is your thorough-bred, gospel-fed man,
Devoted to serving the Lord from his birth,
And surely he'll work for all that he's worth.
    But the Levite fought shy
    And passed stealthily by,
While the chap by the wayside gave vent to a sigh
That ought to have stirred up the angels on high,
And the man in the moon which had lately arisen,
Was led to inquire from his lunary prison
    If that was a test
    Of a saint's very best,
In the care that they take of the weak and oppressed?

But what piratical craft comes here
On a beast with exceeding length of ear,
Whose rider looked more like a buccaneer
Than a man who serves his God in fear?
    No Levite or priest,
    To say the least,
But a man with a heart for even a beast,

Though he came of a tribe that the lordly Jew
Had always snubbed without ado.
Yet he certainly took in a Christian view,
For he clothed the fellow from hat to shoe,
And he mended his bones and patched his mug,
And lifted him on to the long-eared plug,
And dropped him in at the next hotel,
With orders to stop until sound and well,
And what to us is more wonderful still,
He left the money to foot the bill.

Now please don't say my story is thin,
And you don't see where the point comes in,
    For there's surely a hint
    Of a lesson in't,
That a fellow might see with half a squint,
And this is the hint—that I and you
Might preach and pray till all was blue,
And yet if we didn't wake up and do,
We never should get our ticket through.
A hint—and here *our* joy comes in,—
That even the so-called child of sin
May plod along through thick and thin,
Without so much as a hope to win,
    Yet find his place
    At the end of the race,
Mapped out in a most desirable space,
    While those who mix
    In pious tricks
May possibly get into such a fix,
That, be they ever so much devout,
They'll find themselves clean counted out.

There's no end to the hints that one may read
In the Good Samaritan's kindly deed,
    But, strange to say,
    The church of to-day
Has grown so sadly out of joint,
It almost fails to see the point,
And many a heretic, "dyed in the wool,"
Can give its religion an awful pull.

Perhaps my rhyme may meet the eye
Of some who've laid their Bible by,
    Because, forsooth,
    The real truth
Has been garbled in form so very uncouth;
    Yet, my doubting friend,
    It is safe to depend
That justice will certainly come in the end,
    And justice, you know,
    Is giving a show
To a man as far as his merits may go;
    And as none are all pure,
    So none are quite sure
That religion will work them a permanent cure;
    And as none are all evil,
    It may be the devil
Will eventually find himself off of his level,
While "my neighbor," to use a plain figure of speech,
May be sinner or saint, or a little of each.

The Parson's Story.

Good Parson H. had a happy way
Of clinching whatever he had to say,
    With a story or fable,
    From which one was able
    To better determine
    The point of his sermon;
And one Sunday morning he dwelt on the beauty
Of making a practical business of duty;
And he hammered it home and he clinched the last nail,
By relating this simple illustrative tale.

One Mr. Blank, (he gave no name,
But the moral can be deduced the same,)
Was one of a numerous lot of chaps
Who are fond of their Sunday morning naps.
Six days he labored "like all possessed,"
And often quite into the day of rest,
    So when Sunday came
    With its peaceful claim,
He made a late nap a special aim,
Expecting of course that the neighboring chime
Would bring him to life by service time.

But nature is fickle at times, you know,
And our best laid schemes may prove "no go,"
    And Blank, poor fellow,
    Stuck fast to his pillow,
Regardless of future weal or woe,
And when he awakened, it chanced his fate
To be, as he put it, "confoundedly late."
But Blank was quite too much of a saint
To yield the case in despair or complaint,
So he hurriedly rigged his person out
In the Sabbath garb so prim and devout—
The long-tailed coat and stove-pipe hat,
The choker collar and white cravat,
    And the various cues
    Which some would use
To denote they are standing in saintly shoes,
But which practical men will rather choose
To interpret a sort of pious ruse
That is much less apt to deceive than amuse,
And he started off for the neighboring church
Determined not quite to be left in the lurch.
    But Heaven defend
    Our tardy friend,
For with all the speed that his will could lend,
He only succeeded in reaching the place,
To meet the worshippers face to face;
And making up to the nearest one,
Said he—"My friend, is the service done?"
"Oh! no," said the friend with a Christian glow,
"It never will all be *done*, you know;

The service has only been read and sung
With a little send-off by the preacher's tongue.
    It's an easy thing
    To preach and sing
And aim your shots at the bird on the wing,
But as for the business being *done*,
Why, friend, it has only just *begun*."

You see the point the parson made—
That sermons preached and prayers prayed;
That anthems sung with musical quirks
And other so-called devotional works;—
That serving the Master alone by these;
Is simply a fraud or a farce, as you please,
And one might be pardoned, the parson thinks,
For taking his forty morning winks,
And even neglecting the Sunday talk,
If he served the Lord in his daily walk.
    The moral seems plain,
    Though it may not obtain
A hold on the Pharisaically vain,
    But we venture to say
    That the world some day
Will hold, as a final conclusion, at length,
That prayer, minus work, is a waste of strength.

"More Blessed to Give than to Receive."

A solid truth; the very word of God;
Divinely edifying; grandly broad,
   And suited to the use of any creed,
And he who finds no better use for pelf
Than hedging in his egotistic self,
   Must in his soul be very poor indeed.

No figure this of vain bombastic speech
Set for your pedant clergyman to preach,
   That he may beat the air with empty sound;
No blatant, oratoric platitude,
So easy aired, but seldom understood,
   With which your glowing texts so much abound,

But earnest, living truth; a world of bliss
Can come to those who make their Heaven of this,
   Ignoring theologic time and space,
And never cup was pressed to thirsty lip
That he who gave it did not richly sip
   A sweeter draught of sweetest Christian grace.

And though one never kneels at other shrine,
Or worships forms so oft mis-called divine,
   Yet carries comfort to a sorrowing heart;
To him no less is due a just reward
Than if he daily called upon the Lord
   With poor pretence to act the better part.

An Old Story Revised.

A worthy deacon, zealously inspired
    To serve his Master on the doubtful plan
That formal homage was the need required,
    Rather than deeds of love to fellow-man ;
Returning home from church one morning found
A homeless vagrant stretched upon the ground,
And, fresh from exhortation of the word,
A new emotion in his heart was stirred,
Bidding him play the kindly friend in need,
And prove a Good Samaritan indeed.
And so he bade the luckless stranger come
For a brief shelter to his hearth and home.

And now behold our Christian of the schools
    Breaking the bread of life to hungry souls ;
Not greatly trammeled he by golden rules,
    As to the traveler scraps and crumbs he doles :—
Feeding the body that he might prelude
A draught upon the stranger's gratitude,
But representing love, we grieve to say,
In a most meagre, patronizing way,
As if the appetite so long repressed,
Might suffer by a too indulgent zest.

The stranger, thankful even for the least,
Was dealt the poorest morsels of the feast,
And, at the last, as the dessert passed by,
Received the acutest angle of the pie.

And now says the good host, with reverent air,
Hast ever meekly bowed thy head in prayer?
No? Then I'll teach thee how to fitly say
"Our Father"—He to whom in Heaven we pray.
"Our Father,"—says the stranger in amaze;
Is such the name to which the Christian prays?
"Our Father," did you say—both mine and yours?
Why, that my right of brotherhood insures,
And, pray excuse me, but a light breaks in;
If we are really so near of kin,
Dear Christian brother, is it more than fair
To bring this new relationship to bear,
And recognize the bond 'twixt you and I
By giving me a larger share of pie!

Done on Both Sides.

Blue Monday found the parson wan and worn,—
    In that unhappy, fretful state of mind,
Where common mortals doubtless would have sworn,
    And thus profanely left their cares behind:
Not so the parson; he must patient bear
His burdens, with no safety-valve of swear,
Save the rude growling which we worldlings call
About the worst profanity of all.
And so we find him with lugubrious face,
Bewailing the misfortunes of his case,
Unmindful of the fact that burdens fall
In divers shapes and different times on all.
A friend and neighbor listening to his plaint,
Sought to console the sad and suffering saint,
By hints that laymen likewise bore their share
Of Sunday's burden, with its wear and tear.
The parson in amazement raised his eyes,
And viewed his friend and neighbor with surprise;
" 'Tis yours to rest, good brother, while I preach
And rack my brain for proper thought and speech;
Your round of Sabbath duties holds no call
To work from morn till evening shadows fall."
The layman listened in respectful way,
To all the worthy parson chose to say,
And then in kindly tone of mild reproach,
Ventured a different phase of thought to broach,—
"Granted the preacher's toil beyond all doubt,
Yet one important fact he's counted out:

You do the preaching, but you quite forget
The weary listeners who sit and fret,
And all too often, you may rest assured,
We, more than you, have suffered and endured."

Two lessons may the reader here deduce:—
One for the parson for his special use,—
To wit,—that though he labor e'er so hard,
And preach, as he supposes, by the card,
Not all the eloquence his tongue can use
May head off weariness within the pews,
And in the question of a Sabbath rest,
'Tis not unlikely that he fares the best.

But not alone does preacher fail to read
The best interpretation of his creed;
And here comes in our Lesson Number Two,
Which bears directly upon me and you;
Let us remember in our weary mood,
The waste of time in which we fret and brood;—
That there are no exemptions in the plan
Which places burdens upon every man,
And that he best enjoys his honors won,
Who laughs at care and has his honest fun.
Let parsons lay their burdens on their shelves,
And keep their petty troubles to themselves,
And laymen so conduct their daily walk
That there may be less need of Sabbath talk.
Something like this, we think may help to prove
How much of weariness we might remove;
The world would surely be more joyous then,
And even parsons might be better men.

A QUERY.

Who calls his life a failure; have you thought
   How cruel and unjust the charge might be?
Has all your long experience never taught
That many battles may be bravely fought,
   Which do not lead to open victory?—

That staunchest virtues wage a losing fight
   On this uneven battle-ground of doom;
And sterling worth may never come to light,
So deeply shadowed in the gloom of night,
   That heaven alone its presence can illume.

And this poor fellow, gone at last to rest,
   His life enclouded e'er it had begun;
Can you not hope that he has done his best
With the small gifts of which he was possessed,
   And what could highest manhood more have done?

And you his judge? you, who have never known
   An hour of real care to haunt your mind,
Who bade you take on this censorious tone,
Assuming that your little world alone
   Held all the virtue of the gods combined?

O 'tis an easy thing for Fortune's pet
    To patronize the weak beneath his feet;
To wear the supercilious coronet
(For which, by birth or chance, he lives in debt,)
    That crowns the kingdom of a fool's conceit.

Then spare your cold contempt all undeserved;
    It has no place beside this humble grave;
Cleaner his record, though he may have swerved,
Than that of men who only better served,
    Because their Maker richer talents gave.

Heaven credits us, we trust, with our intent,
    And not with every weak and stumbling fall;
Else could we understand but little meant
When speaking of the care beneficent,
    That in His Providence, is showered on all.

God our poor judgments often will reverse,
    Interpreting our failures as success.
He placed us here for better and for worse,
And though some lives may seem to hold a curse,
    Yet each can have its little power to bless.

Goose Egg Hatched Out.

"Little Jack Horner
Sat in the corner," &c.—*Mother Goose.*

From legend or fable
The preacher is able
To cook up a dish that will garnish his table,
And the text we have quoted
May well be devoted
To airing a streak for which some men are noted.
There are plenty of fellows about us to day,
Who tackle their pie in a Horner-like way,
And Horner the first
Is by no means the worst
Of the Horners with which we are sadly accursed.
The creature of fable is quite hid from sight
By Horners that knock him as high as a kite,
And the grip of the thumb
Which they put on the plum,
Would strike the plain amateur pie-eater dumb.
With an evident air
Of a "deuced if they care
Whether any one else shall come in for a share,"

   Poor you and poor I
   Might stand hungrily by
Without getting even a smell of the pie.

The Horner of old was mythic and vague;
The Jack of to-day is a positive plague,
   That ought to be missed,
   But contrives to exist,
To illustrate the possible use of a curse,
By comparing the bad with what might have been worse.
Oh! Horner, old chap, if you only but knew
What awful hard things folks are saying of you;
If you only could hear the unpleasant remarks
That crop out in discussing of ravenous sharks;
Unless you've a conscience remarkably spry,
You would lose half the relish of eating your pie.
There's a Scriptural hint that an oven is heating,
Where the "very old Horner" will cook for his eating,
   And his pie—don't forget it,—
   (You'll know when he's ate it,)
Will be brim-full of such plums as you, if you let it,
   And when you shall die,
   Unless epitaphs lie,
On your tombstone shall read,"What a mean wretch was I."

   Now Jack of the story
   Felt quite "hunki-dori,"
As he sat in conceited and conscious self glory,
   Yet somehow or other,
   You or I it might bother,
To act quite so much like a pig's elder brother,

   And there might come a feeling
   That that kind of dealing
In decent men's eyes seemed the next door to stealing,
So if ever it strikes you as something quite nice,
To devour all your pie, never leaving a slice,
   You'd better think twice
   Of the selfish device
Before selling out at so narrow a price,
   And scatter a plum
   From the liberal sum
That the Fates may have kindly placed under your thumb,
   And whenever you feed,
   Pray don't in your greed,
Forget your poor neighbor in pitiful need,
   But pass your pie round
   And the writer'll be bound
That the seed of your plums will spring up in good ground,
   Bearing fruit every day
   That will fully repay
For the labor and sacrifice given away.

PHILOSOPHIC SALAD,

COMPOUNDED OF

SUNDRY CRUSTS AND CRUMBS.

Local Philosophy.

What is Philosophy but common sense
Adjusted to the ways of Providence?

Better than all your philanthropic talks,
Are ashes scattered over icy walks.

Trying to serve at once both God and Mammon,
We're credibly informed, is purely gammon.

Good neighborhoods owe much to common sense,
Backed up by patience and a high board-fence.

"Nothing is lost," exclaim some owl-like "fellers;"
Then where on earth are all my old umbrellas?

Next to a lack of brain comes lack of thought:
Men give this less attention than they ought.

Unwilling charity at best will seem
Like milk of human kindness, robbed of cream.

In spite of all the poet dreams or sings,
God's real angels move with feet, not wings.

The law of compensation carries double;
Your fun may represent another's trouble.

Develop bumps of jollity and mirth
And work your happiness for all its worth.

He that expects to clearly solve Life's riddle,
Might just as well hang up his bow and fiddle.

We often wonder—will the world of bliss
Have any better show for us than this.

Whether to-day be wreathed with smiles or tears,
But little matters in a thousand years.

Make, while you can, the most of youthful joys;
Old age trips up the liveliest of the boys.

Ah! friend, the things we ought to value most,
Are never fairly prized till they are lost.

How few of us have not in some way sung
That good old tune of "Go it while you're young."

Don't boast of your apparent luck too soon;
To-morrow you may sing a different tune.

Anticipation will quite often bless
More than reality, and costs much less.

Youth builds its castles from most stunning plans
And sets in motion gorgeous caravans;

Old age, from out the shaky castle wall,
Has seen the elephant and that is all.

The "cussedness" of man, we grieve to say,
Has often pushed Heaven's choicest gifts away.

Let well enough alone; don't fret and fuss
Because the good things don't all come to us.

He is a Christian who can daily wear
A mask of cheer to hide a life of care.

If our designs were not sometimes defeated,
The human animal would grow conceited.

Because your wish was vain, don't feel distressed;
"What can't be cured must be"—you know the rest.

Love in a cottage, with baked beans for two,
Discounts a palace with its gold and blue.

A healthy proverb—"Look before you leap;"
'Twill save you landing in a garbage heap.

We don't suppose that Heaven ever meant
That we should settle down in pure content.

It can't be long before we slip away;
Let's take a little comfort while we may.

Why do they always wait till we are dead
Before they let their words of praise be said?

Don't fool on slippery ground; with proper care
A man stays right end up most anywhere.

It mostly happens that the man of brag
Pulls at a heavier load than he can drag.

No man not tested has a right to say
How much temptation he can put away.

As years go by, old chap, the chance increases
That your philosophy will fall to pieces.

The driest turf upon a barren heath
May hide a rich bonanza underneath.

A waste of time—to scour up souls on Sunday
And drag them in the dirt again on Monday.

Why fish for heathen on a foreign shore,
When hosts of unconverted live next door?

In striving lesser joys and sweets to taste,
We let life's real pleasures go to waste.

Brains have a tone of good repute about them,
But lots of fellows scrub along without them.

"Remember to keep well the Sabbath Day;"
This doesn't mean—"give other days away."

Why was not Life all happiness and fun?
We give it up; give us an easier one.

He is no friend who careless lets us stray
Into some wicked and forbidden way.

Hard fact and sentiment may often vary;
Tombstones can lie like sin, but figures—"nary."

In serving others stand upon your rights;
Don't act as tails for other people's kites.

"All is not gold that glitters;" this accounts
For sundry frauds and spurious amounts.

I've ever noticed that the loudest scoffer
Has seldom had a better thing to offer.

Keep cool, young man; there's nothing gained by worrying,
And many races have been lost by hurrying.

See to it, friend, that all your loud professing,
Drops in your pathway little seeds of blessing.

Before you count a wayward brother out,
Give him the benefit of every doubt.

Ten-cent cigars and constant swigs of beer,
Absorb a heap of money in a year.

The level-headed man will not dispute
With one who wears a larger size of boot.

Diplomacy, dear friend, is largely tact
In making humbug serve the place of fact.

Men conquer giant oaks with mighty rush,
Yet get all tangled in the underbrush.

'Tis possible with ample moral tone,
To have a little heaven of your own.

We find our neighbors full of moral taints,
While we of course are embryotic saints.

Who curbs the tongue, will find, to say the least,
They're harnessing a very curious beast.

Some are content, howe'er the Fates decree it;
"All's for the best," they say, but I can't see it.

You'll aim to smother trouble if you're wise;
Small griefs, if harped on, swell to mountain size.

Be ever helpful; they who highest roost,
Climb all the better for a gentle "boost."

"Childlike" and "bland"—two taffy-laden phrases,—
Applied to ways that may mislead like blazes.

A soothing syrup for the truly humble—
When they slip up they haven't far to tumble.

Tears dropped in spilled milk only weaken more
The lacteal that was all too thin before.

How much of honesty is true and candid,
Or how much may be fairly termed left-handed?

Who spends beyond his income drifts to want;
A solid fact—that "two from one you can't."

The human mule, for stupidity, can beat
His quadrupedal namesake every heat.

Frown not on aspirants for fame and honor;
The man without ambition is a "goner."

One over-zealous friend may work more ill
Than twenty active enemies can will.

No rule of conduct answers for us all;
Coats that fit me may prove for you too small.

Doubtless it proves a blessing to some men,
To have a little set-back now and then.

There's no philosophy we've ever tried,
Which for the back and stomach could provide.

One sin doth many virtues counteract;—
This is not poetry but bottom fact.

Young man, remember that your worthy dad
Works from experience you haven't had.

They tell us that hard luck developes men,
And yet we are not happy even then.

Will some one tell us why the ripest peach
Forever grows the farthest from our reach.

A maxim paradoxical in kind :—
"Go slow"—it seldom leaves one far behind.

If half our recollections were "forgets,"
'Twould leave unborn our bitterest regrets.

There is no friendship which can stand the wear
Of drafts made any time and everywhere.

The poorest scallawag that passes by,
Is just as much God's child as you or I.

The doors of opportunity are wide;
Don't say you can't get in before you've tried.

Take off your hat to merit where you find it,
Regardless of the poverty behind it.

Fractions are vulgar, but however small,
Give us the fraction if we can't have all.

He that is born a day behind the times,
Seldom to any high position climbs.

Wisdom from Folly doth but little differ;—
A few years older grown and somewhat stiffer.

Of many evils choose the least, though then
We'll bet a hat you'd like to choose again.

It would be something quite unique and nice
If people sometimes took their own advice.

In this poor life where much must needs go ill,
The cheerful man fills an important bill.

He is the true philosopher who makes
A seeming blessing grow from his mistakes.

Don't count the man with sober phiz a bear;
Warm hearts may throb beneath a look of care.

Quite unavoidable—in stating facts,
One often deals out most unfriendly whacks.

How some chaps come by all their high priced clothes,
Heaven and the unpaid tailor only knows.

Forbidden fruit, though sweet, we think you'll find
Decays much sooner than the other kind.

In judging others, labor to be fair;
We can't tell what we'd do if we were there.

Some folks are born for luck; they hit the mark,
Though shooting ne'er so blindly in the dark.

Count fifty when you feel inclined to swear;
'Twill cool you off and purify the air.

Though eight quarts make a peck by book or sum,
One makes a peck—of trouble (if it's rum.)

We find it edifying to observe
How little men expect what they deserve.

The market rate of every man depends
Upon the good opinion of his friends.

Friend, for an honest blunder feel not sore;
Who does his best can surely do no more.

A huge mistake;—to under-rate your foe;
Who does it lets one half his chances go.

The world has yet to learn that any laurels
Have ever grown from vict'ries won in quarrels.

Philosophers are men who never fret,
But specimens are very rare as yet;

Female philosophers, therefore you see,
Must ever be an unknown quantity.

We're finding out by very slow degrees,
That men can't gather figs from thistle trees.

It isn't every one who comprehends
The value of the little odds and ends.

Our dread is not so much of sin, I fear,
As that our slip may reach somebody's ear.

How it would brighten Life's tempestuous weather
If everybody only pulled together.

Some people never ripen; they're as green
At seventy-five as when they were sixteen.

A consolation staunch and water-tight;—
In Heaven's plan, "Whatever is, is right."

It often happens that the biggest muddle
Comes from the smallest toad that stirs the puddle.

Take any side that's backed by common sense,
But don't for goodness' sake sit on the fence.

Both good and ill from the same threads are spun;
The bee makes honey, but he stings like fun.

A straw for those whose hope needs resurrecting,—
Things pan out well when we are least expecting.

Whatever is inherited adheres;
"Silk purses are not made from porcine ears."

No true politeness ever made it proper
To flatter with a taffy-laden whopper.

Sarcasm catches hold where logic fails,
And sharply handled, drives some clinching nails.

When rogues approve of what you say and do,
Isn't it time to stop and start anew.

Some people never rate a project high,
Unless they have a finger in the pie.

"What folks might say," is the Satanic charm
That bolsters up a deal of needless harm.

Beware of small mistakes; a trifling blunder,
In spite of all your strength may drag you under.

Sharp bargains play the mischief with the heart,
And ought not to be reckoned in as smart.

Place proper value on your good old mother;
When she pegs out you can't scare up another.

The swine lack one accomplishment of man;
They cannot use tobacco and we can.

When all at once the wicked man grows kind,
Depend upon it he's an axe to grind.

Through sheer neglect we drift into a pickle,
And then we whine at Fortune being fickle.

Unless a man has got an iron system,
It won't take long for alcohol to twist him.

Nature assigns each living thing its right;
Dogs have their day and cats about all night.

A constant saving of a dime a day,
In years to come may keep the wolf away.

The best society, blue-blood or not,
Often pans out a miscellaneous lot.

He who expects to take in all he hears,
Must build an annex to enlarge his ears.

Some men forget more in an hour or two,
Than others in a life time ever knew.

My lazy friend, take this advice on trust:—
The bread of idleness is largely crust.

Truth epitaphic—"Ceased from earthly labors,
She rests in peace," and—also do her neighbors.

For men to build too much upon self-glory,
Betokens weakness in the upper story.

Brains do not come at will, though kings command it;
He that is born a fool has got to stand it.

They say sea-sickness has its healthy side;
It can't be any that we ever tried.

The man so hard that sorrow will not soften,
Can't say his prayers too early or too often.

Surprises catch us in so many ways,
Philosophy goes begging now-a-days.

Haste with glad tidings, but be slow with news,
The tone of which can only wound or bruise.

The gift of life is shamefully abused;
More time is wasted than is ever used.

Even a ghost might be induced to laugh;—
To read the lies that cram his epitaph.

When one's salvation is a thing of doubt,
Don't ask his politics but pull him out.

Men who are starving can't afford to question
What is or is not proper for digestion.

Pride as a sauce, has in it much of savor,
But as an entire meal is not in favor.

Satan contrives to pull on every wire
That runs a toasting fork into his fire.

'Tis mighty handy as a sort of blind,
To say you've left your pocket-book behind.

Take note that men who climb ambition's ladder,
Most always slide down wiser men and sadder.

Seeming Humility may ape its guise,
Just to throw dust in other people's eyes.

While you are telling of "what can't be done,"
Another scores the innings at a run.

What passes current as profound astuteness,
Is often nothing but spasmodic cuteness.

'Twere better for the weak and chicken-hearted
If their terrestrial car had never started.

You need not fear that an excess of virtue,
Will ever come in quantities to hurt you.

There is a proverb somewhere in the books,
That puts good conduct quite beyond good looks.

That blamed idea of rising with the lark,
Sprung from some wooden-headed patriarch.

Let not old people sneer at childish ways;
All geese were goslings in their younger days.

Custom will reconcile a man to uses,
That once he looked upon as grave abuses.

Pay all your honest debts before you try
To put on airs and live in luxury.

Book learning has its use, but common sense
Will pass (parse) without the aid of mood or tense.

The good will of the meanest curs that yelp,
May some day prove a very useful help.

Let those who small beginnings would despise,
Study the story of an acorn's rise.

Heaven has no room for worries or complaints,
No grumblers are transmogrified to saints.

Where the shoe pinches none so well can say,
As he who limps in torment day by day.

The man whose heart is wedded to his dimes,
Will make his future home in tropic climes.

"The good die young:"—therefore we may conclude
That you and I are anything but good.

A dainty stomach can't afford to look
Too closely at the methods of the cook.

Lotteries, my friend, are wicked and unwise,
Unless your ticket chance to draw a prize.

Stiff upper-lip and amplitude of cheek
Brace up some chaps who are confounded weak.

The record of no man is quite so clear
As not to furnish food for gossip's ear.

People endowed with gab must not forget
That hasty speech gives birth to much regret.

Don't aim too large a portion to control;
Who grasps too much, perchance may lose the whole.

His is a poor excuse whose lack of thought,
Alone shall plead his case should he be caught.

It isn't safe for any one to bet
That all the fools are dead and buried yet:—

While men rate human wisdom, so to speak,
By loud profession and extent of cheek;

While Fortune's drones cast idiotic snub
On honest toilers for their daily grub;

When common sense good people so much lack,
They starve the stomach to adorn the back;

While dolts, oblivious to the risk they run,
Would solve the problem of a loaded gun,

Or in her careless haste, a kitchen queen
Climbs Heavenward by the aid of kerosene;

While men are found so ready to endorse
For those who ride a lame financial horse,

Or others, blindly stupid, recommend
An arrant scoundrel for a worthy friend,

Or think to play the game of politics,
By counting any honors with the tricks:—

While things like these are rife, we're free to say—
"The fools are not all dead and packed away."

The world is moving, friend; if you don't mind,
The train will start and you'll be left behind.

Whene'er we see the head ignore the heart,
We think there's such a thing as being too smart.

Candor is quite desirable, but pray
Don't give quite all you think or know away.

Act for yourself; this doing things by proxy,
Is worthy of the lazy and the foxy.

Take not to heart the scoldings of a friend;
True love may chide, but never should offend.

With what we have we seldom are content,
But always long for blessings never sent.

In calculating chances, always make
A due allowance for an unseen break.

A proper rule for greedy ones to follow;—
Never to bite off more than they can swallow.

An ounce of wise prevention, so they say,
Is worth a dozen doctors any day.

Happy the man who can philosophize
That all his woes are blessings in disguise.

Work out your own salvation; don't depend
Upon that doubtful quantity, your friend.

The veriest rascal may give good advice;
He bought his wisdom at the highest price.

A hint for general use;—he is a dunce,
Who thinks to occupy two stools at once.

Young man, the time will come, depend upon it,
When you are sure to wish you hadn't done it.

What is sweet music for one man to hear,
Is pandemonium to another's ear.

Heaven's blessing rest with him who stamps a veto
On that tormenting nuisance, the mosquito.

A dollar earned buys more of real Heaven,
Than twenty dollars that are idly given.

King Solomon was level when he said—
"Look not upon the wine when it is red."

Apologies sometimes act like a curse,
And serve to make the previous question worse.

Before you marry use deliberate thought;
Too late to reconsider when you're caught.

Strive not to know too much, rather be sure
That what you do know is the Simon-pure.

Our zeal and interest is largest shown
In everybody's business but our own.

'Tis better to arise an hour too soon,
Than take your breakfast in the afternoon.

Repenting under fire is rather thin;
The Lord is not so easy taken in.

Go very slow; then, if you jump the track,
You'll stand a better chance of working back.

Imagination plays a powerful hand
In wafting Fancy's sails to real land.

A glaring weakness; to be self-deceived;
We often glory when we should have grieved.

The world has room enough, kind Heaven knows,
Without our treading on each other's toes.

Christians are born, not made; we find that out
By passing contribution plates about.

'Tis quite astounding how some chaps get on,
With all their capital and credit gone.

Don't hope to squelch a courtship by abuse;
Where hearts are trumps, clubs are of little use.

Were wisdom born with our advancing years,
Old age would wear more smiles and fewer tears.

A picture of contentment hard to match;—
A full blown darkey in a melon patch.

Bad luck the day when Adam lost his head,
And made us fellows toil and sweat for bread.

Experience proves it neither safe nor wise
To argue with a man that's twice your size.

Self-praise may be a weakness to regret,
But then you know, 'tis all some fellows get.

Among your luxuries, include old boots;
They show up comfort to its very roots.

Man's appetite will always take the lead;
The babe's first cry is solid for its feed.

Wise is that man who waiteth for his smile,
Till he has landed safely o'er the stile.

Though cynics grind their epigrams at will,
The world clings to its own opinions still.

In happiest hours are hidden bitter pills,
The feast that gorges breeds the pain that kills.

Modern extravagance has no defence
In running things regardless of expense:

A third-class coach will take you just as far
As though you traveled in a palace car;

Fine clothes will decorate a dudish form,
But homespun cloth will keep you just as warm;

Plain bread and milk will make a fellow fatter
Than high-priced game or oysters fried in batter.

We have this hopeful thought to lay away,—
That people don't mean half of what they say.

Old fashioned honesty is hard to beat;
Candor is better than polite deceit.

Mirth is a medicine and they who laugh,
Postpone to some extent, their epitaph.

Man's inconsistency his conduct trammels;
He strains at gnats and swallows fearful camels.

The mud and mire of life is deep, 'tis true;
But better men than we have waded through.

A very slight indulgence now and then,
Has played the mischief with the best of men.

Those who must dance will find out to their sorrow—
The fiddler's bill must be paid on the morrow.

An argument to hang up on a peg:—
"Which started first, the chicken or the egg?"

"Gone to the bad:" the usual verdict given,
When some poor chap has missed the way to Heaven.

If you have stingy children, blame yourself;
It shows their daddy had a love for pelf.

No man so low but he may rise, perhaps,
And none so lofty but he may collapse.

'Twould scarce be deemed a true parental merit,
To flog a child for what he might inherit.

Sail in, my boy, and take the foremost chance,
If you desire to see the monkey dance.

One man will careless throw into the fire,
What to another is his heart's desire.

At other's faults and failings spare your jokes;
Your wheel may have some loose and cranky spokes.

Pigs are not all four-legged; not a few
Contrive to get about quite well on two.

Because our Uncle Adam acted rash,
We can't quite think the world is going to smash.

Here is a fact, though some won't comprehend it:—
Nursing a trouble never helps to mend it.

"Fine feathers make fine birds," yet none the less,
A bird may sweetly sing in plainest dress.

Let those who think we're moving rather slow,
Compare to-day with fifty years ago.

No one who scans the market can deny
That first-class men are very scarce and high.

Friend, do not cheat thyself with the conceit,
That all the brains are traveling on thy feet.

If Hell is paved with good intents caved in,
The writer claims a right of way therein.

When in grave doubt switch off and change the tune;
You cannot leave disputed ground too soon.

Memories are mental insects armed with stings,
That follow in our wake with tireless wings.

That most men have their price we may not doubt;
But how confounded cheap they all sell out!

As well try cooling Tophet with a fan,
As using reason with an angry man.

Lack of ambition cheapens human worth,
In any market on this bustling earth.

Sooner or late in every man's career,
He squeezeth out the penitential tear.

Don't fish for fortune with a sudden jerk;
The patient plodder gets in solid work.

"Provide things honest:"—a remark of Paul,
Who took no stock in tricky fol-de-rol.

"Not lost but gone before:"—a pleasant manner
Of stating what the matter was with Hannah.

I like that text which says—"Friend, come up higher;"
It catches on to those down in the mire.

The world existed ere you came to town,
And will move on when you are salted down.

The baldest fact, shown in an honest light,
Knocks all your theories higher than a kite.

Cure for insomnia:—hire a cushioned pew,
And use it Sundays for a month or two.

Need we sulk off and play a game of dumps,
Because our cards don't always turn up trumps?

Repentance doesn't make as good as new;
We've tried it on and know this to be true.

You can't judge business by the splurge that's made;
Hens often cackle when they haven't laid.

Never exaggerate; if you must lie,
Explode the facts and blow the truth sky-high.

Give out that some poor chap has missed his bearing,
And all the world will give the tale an airing.

Haste does not always guarantee completeness;
The fruit that soonest ripens lacks in sweetness.

Draughts from an open window play the deuce
With folks whose cog-wheels are a little loose.

Beware, young men and maidens; greatest catches
May often prove to be the sorriest matches.

In the long run, simplicity of heart
Will win more friendship than deceitful art.

Reject apologies, as any goose
Can conjure up some sort of an excuse.

How meanly must some men regard their souls,
To squeeze them through such fearfully small holes.

No one seemed better fixed than Father Adam,
Yet blessings slipped him when he thought he had 'em.

No doctors have been able to invent
An antidote to head off discontent.

God never meant for you, on state occasions,
To turn your nose up at your poor relations.

Our hands may work more mischief in a day,
Than all eternity can clear away.

How does it always happen in a fuss,
That everybody is to blame but us.

Don't waste your strength in idiotic schemes,
Born of wild nightmares and dyspeptic dreams.

Who feed on hopes need neither beg nor starve;
There's always one upon the board to carve.

The smallest speck located in one's eye,
May cloud a twenty acre lot of sky.

The man who stubs his toe and doesn't swear,
Can be relied on for an honest prayer.

Behold, how all the rabble of the town
Will pitch into a fellow when he's down.

We haven't long to stay; let's do our part,
So people won't shout "Glory" when we start.

Never forget in boasting of descent,
That birth is but the merest accident.

Truth never moves in complicated tracks;
Children and fools get very near the facts.

Some tears are no more kin to real grief,
Than pure tobacco to a cabbage leaf.

A deal of time is spent in picking flaws,
That might be worked into a better cause.

He who in business is unjustly sharp,
Will never play upon a Heavenly harp.

Don't borrow trouble for the coming day;
The present penance is enough to pay.

A little nonsense mingled with our toil,
Acts like a dose of lubricating oil.

"Let Satan have his due;"—we argue thus,
But what the dickens would become of us?

Men of small gifts should not discouraged be;
It was a mouse that set the lion free.

"Be wise in time;"—which means—don't go it blind,
And everlastingly come in behind.

Console yourself in trouble with this thought;—
You don't get half the punishment you ought.

Fortune coquettes in ways both rare and pleasing;
Some take the snuff while others do the sneezing.

Successful financiering now consists
In giving creditors the various twists.

Bluster and Brag will never fill the bill;
" 'Tis the still swine that gobble up the swill."

In seeking great things, ne'er despise the less;
It's but a step 'twixt failure and success.

Vice only needs a little virtuous paint,
To make a sinner seem a finished saint.

Historic records amply testify
That good men can act naughty—on the sly.

A crumb of consolation for the poor—
They easier lift the latch to Heaven's door.

The hand of Providence takes on a grip
That is not prone to let its business slip.

Hope spins a thread that somehow catches on,
Long after every real chance is gone.

God was the architect who planned this earth;
This is a hint to those who doubt its worth.

Bury your hates; this life is all too brief
To have its pleasure marred by needless grief.

Columbus had a very faint idea
Of what a "show" he started over here.

Hope is perennial, else the poor old heart
Would shrink and dry up till it fell apart.

Your hearty eater seldom waxeth fat;
How do the scientists account for that?

The good we do will help but precious little
The evil part of our account to settle.

Knowledge is not all taught by book or school;
We may learn wisdom even from a fool.

SOBERER RHYMES.

1—Leaves from Life.
2—Retrospective.
3—Contentment.
4—A Life's Record.
5—Not Boasting, but Hopeful.
6—To the Skeptic.
7—A Suggestion.
8—Life's Mystery.
9—A Skeleton in every Closet.
10—Of What Avail?
11—Vain Glory.
12—Our World.

LEAVES FROM LIFE.

I—LONGING.

"We spend our years but as a tale that's told,"
   And poor humanity has ever striven
   To lift its little world-life nearer Heaven
By weaving in its web some threads of gold.
And though the plot is drawn with master skill
   And wise design is stamped on every page,
Like some poor bird, the fettered human will
   Chafes in the narrow limits of its cage.
The babe with tiny hand would grasp the moon;
   The boy and girl in air their castles build,
And even man, in life's gray afternoon,
   Its sunset rays a brighter hue would gild.
Thus runs the story through the ages past;
So must it ever read unto the last.

II—EXPERIENCE

Mysterious volume! writ in foreign tongue,
   With no translating hand which holds the key;
   The why and wherefore of our destiny
Has never yet been clearly read or sung,

We only know—(ah! know we not too much?)—
　　That not again in any coming year,
Shall hover quite so near the infant's touch,
　　The glittering bauble it had held so dear.
We know the youth and maid shall build in vain,
　　Their fabric melting into dust and tears,
While of Life's day-dreams, little shall remain
　　To light the pilgrim down the vale of years.
And this, so far as we can see or know,
Will close the book to mortals here below.

III—HOPE.

But from the cravings of the human soul,
　　Another volume has been long foretold,
　　In radiant garb of mingled blue and gold,
A fitting end and sequel to the whole:
And here the Author of this life of ours,—
　　This tangled web with many a broken thread,
From ugliest thorns has culled the sweetest flowers;
　　From darkest pages happiest lessons read.
Here are no youthful longings unfulfilled;
　　No airy castles sadly brought to grief,
And weary hearts may find their pulses thrilled
　　By helpful words that blazon every leaf.
Is it so strange that we should sometimes plead
This final volume of our life to read?

Retrospective.

The years are fleeting fast, O thoughtless one,
    And is your task wrought out?
Have all the honors of a life been won,—
    All errors put to rout?

Was your existence of no greater worth
    Through all the passing hours,
That in the garden which you tilled on earth,
    Sprang up more weeds than flowers?

Can you with open gaze review the past,
    The story of your years,
And read a record with no faults o'ercast,
    A memory with no tears?

Have all the sunny smiles your Fortune brought,
    Your little world improved?
Were care and sorrow hid with kindly thought
    To spare the friend you loved?

And when some weary comrade ceased to run
    And faltered on the road,
Did you do all a brother might have done
    To ease his heavy load?

Was some poor creature tempted—God knows how—
    To leave the path of right,
And yours the hand to lift her from the slough,
    Or crowd her out of sight?

With starving souls on every side who plead
    Only for crumbs, no more,
Were there no hungry ones you might have fed
    From out your bounteous store?

Creation cannot be an idle freak
    Of purposeless caprice,
And Life would be a sorry gift and weak,
    That brought not joy or peace.

Why should not memory as your sun goes down,
    Refresh your fading sight
With scenes that bear no semblance to a frown,
    And pictures of delight?

The years are fleeting fast, O thoughtless one,
    Years that have fled for aye,
But little seeds of good our hands have sown
    Take root and ne'er decay.

CONTENTMENT.

Possess thy soul in patience, troubled one:
   Thou canst not if thou would, have perfect peace;
A restless yearning was with life begun,
   That will not give the struggling soul release.
We cherish lofty hopes;—moments there are
   When the whole world would hardly satisfy
   The greedy gaze of an ambitious eye,
That longing, looks beyond the farthest star.
Such moods are vanities of thought,—the dreams
   That ought not if they could, be e'er fulfilled;—
   Tainted with poison that has been distilled
From noxious vapors of unhealthy themes.
God's happiest children are his humblest ones;
   It is not theirs in grief and shame to hide
   The bitter pangs of disappointed pride,
Though each be distanced in the race he runs.
The modest goal toward which their feet may tend
Charms with the grace simplicity can lend,
And sweet humility is amply blest
With the sure promise of a helpful rest.
Not in a life of wild ambition spent,
   Has grown a fruitage on which feeds the soul,
But in the lowlands of a sweet content
   Uplifted here and there with flowery knoll.
The monarch clad in kingly purple, wears
A mask that hides a weary load of cares;
While all his gilded dignity of rank
Reflects and echoes but a mocking blank,

Nor pomp nor pageantry can quite conceal
The human longings that his heart may feel.

Then do not fret the weary hours away,
Waiting the promise of a brighter day;
Thine may not be the only aching heart;
   Another, more than thou, is weighted down,—
Given a load to carry from the start,
   That decked its bearer with a martyr's crown:
And rest thy soul in peace and calm content;
   All things are working for a final good,
And life perhaps, would be more wisely spent
   Were all its hidden purpose understood.

A LIFE'S RECORD.

My years have come and gone; the hours have flown
   That marked my ideal of a perfect life,
   Yet I have little known but toil and strife
That left the toiler weary and alone.
Ah! 'tis a sorry ending to the dreams
With which the youthful fancy richly teems;
Hurled from the airy heights he fain had trod,
With tired feet the rudest path to plod.
My joys were flavored with a bitter-sweet;
   The fruit so full of promise in its bloom,
But fell to dust and ashes at my feet
   And wrapped me round in clouds of doubt and gloom;
And, saddest thought, to learn, alas, too late
What might have led one to a better fate.

NOT BOASTING, BUT HOPEFUL.

'Tis not for us to idly boast
  Of victories won;
Another, though he may have lost,
  Hath braver done.
Ours was a safer path to go;
'Twas his to meet a deadlier foe,
And Heaven alone shall ever know
  The worthier one.

We fought our battle from a height,
  On vantage ground,
While he, poor fellow, in the night,
  Asleep was found.
So should we bear our honors meek,
Nor vaunt our prowess o'er the weak,
But rather may the words we speak
  In grace abound.

We entered for the race, perhaps
  The best equipped;
He at the outset many laps
  Behind had slipped,
Yet need we cling to the advance
With haughty step and scornful glance,
Nor deign to give another chance
  To him who tripped?

One opes his Book of Life at first
  Without a blot;
Another starts almost accurst,
  So hard his lot;

Yet patient toil and honest worth
Can quite redeem the taints of birth,
And shape a better life on earth
    Than he had thought.

Man's lot no wisdom of the schools
    Can quite decide;
But even-handed justice rules
    On every side,
And there shall come a better fate
To those whose souls in patience wait
The certain good that soon or late
    The gods provide.

TO THE SKEPTIC.

Hast ever thought, O thou of cynic tongue,
    Who aimest shafts with such envenomed point,
    Inveighing at a world so out of joint,
That all of Life from the same Hand had sprung—
And that a Master Hand? Cans't thou believe
    That He who filled our lives with joy and light
    Has not within his grasp a power and might
In perfect harmony His plans to weave?
O ye of little faith?—Can ye not trust,
    Reasoning from what ye know, to the unknown?
Wait ye in patient hope because ye must,
    Nor think that God will not protect his own.
Sublime conceit, that rears its puny thought
Where wisest minds have but too feebly taught!

A SUGGESTION.

Carefully, friend, some hearts are very sore
   And quiver at the lightest blow or touch;
   Is it, then, asking of you quite too much,
That you should speak your careless words no more?
See how a sad life feeds on crumbs of Hope
   And how it starves amid a cold disdain;
Note how in solitude the soul will mope,
   Yet won by kindness to its joy again;
And kind words cost so little—while a smile
   Is easier born than scornful word or frown,
Yet half the world seems trying all the while
   To crowd their poorer, weaker neighbors down.
Oh! strange neglect and woful lack of thought;
Was this the lesson that the Master taught?

Carefully, friend, it may be yours some day
   To hear the bitter taunt, the heartless sneer;
   To see the friend that you had deemed sincere,
Turn with a cruel thoughtlessness away.
There is no human lot so fair or grand,
   That may not crumble into baser form;
There is no earthly height where one may stand
   Safe from the sweep of passing blast and storm:
For your own sake, then, would we humbly plead;
   Bread cast upon the waters is not lost,
But may return to us, and richly feed
   The springs of life that suffering would exhaust.
For your own sake as well as for the race,
Let charity your life and conduct grace.

LIFE'S MYSTERY.

We bid our friends "Good-bye;"
We see them crossing to the other shore,
And though we shall not ever greet them more,
    We have no cause to sigh.

We dare not wish them back,
For there is rest, and here a weary round
Of never ending care that knew no bound,
    Beset them on their track.

Need we so selfish seem,
That we can stand beside the open grave
Of our dear friends in peaceful sleep, and crave
    To wake them from their dream?

Is Life so very dear—
So richly glowing with a golden sheen,
That we would longing linger on the scene
    And wish it ever near?

Is there for human eyes,
No fairer land than this domain of ours;
No sweeter music or more fragrant flowers,
    No land of Paradise?

In mystery we hope;
The path into the future is so dark,
Our thoughts are but an endless "hush" and "hark",
So blindly do we grope;

And so we firmly clasp
The little treasure we have learned to love,
Rather than seek for that we know not of,
So far beyond our grasp.

Dear friends for whom we grieve;
A voice the soul alone can understand,
Is telling of a fairer, better land;
We listen and believe,

With firm and tender trust,
That He who guards this life from day to day,
And tempers kindly every earthly way,
Hereafter will be just.

O mystery unsolved,—
How long e'er human prescience reach a height;
From which to see by what decree of right
God's problems are evolved.

A SKELETON IN EVERY CLOSET.

As lurked of old the fabled wraith
  In legend dim,
So strides in every human path
  A spectre grim:
As if a weird, unhallowed sprite
Had crept from out the gloom of night
To exercise by ghostly right,
  Its solemn whim.

It wears the form of shadowy ghosts
  Of mythic woes;
It numbers with its legions hosts
  Of direst foes;
It strikes its terrors on the great
Alike with those of humbler fate,
And travels onward at a rate
  No mortal knows.

It trifles with our fondest hopes
  And mocks in scorn;
In gayest hours it sits and mopes
  With air forlorn;

It cometh like a thief at night
And scatters an unwholesome blight
That clouds our vision to the light
    Of coming dawn.

It shadows all our petted schemes
    Like one possessed;
It harasses our nightly dreams
    And murders rest;
It fills the weary, aching head
With never ending fear and dread
Of things unpleasant done or said
    Which we detest.

It haunts the bonnie bride with fear
    Of coming care;
It whispers in the bridegroom's ear
    Of toil and snare;
It drives the loving parent wild
With anxious thought of wayward child,
Refusing to be reconciled
    In her despair.

And though we place no welcome chair,
    This friend to greet,
He steals upon us unaware
    And takes his seat.
And when we fain in peace would sup,
He calls some horrid vision up
That gives a bitter to the cup
    That should be sweet.

There comes a day of endless shade,
    We humbly trust,
When ghosts and goblins may be laid
    Like forms of dust.
And haunted man so long oppressed
With hopeless visions of unrest,
Shall sleep the sleep assigned the blest,
    Among the just.

OF WHAT AVAIL?

How human life repeats an oft told tale;—
For some rich distant port we set our sail,
But if we founder and the voyage fail,
    Of what avail?

Of what avail the glowing dreams of youth,
If they must realize in forms uncouth,
While all fulfilment in a joyous truth,
    They lack forsooth?

Of what avail a man's ambitious pride,
Towering above all other aims beside,
If, at the last, its ghost sits by his side,
    But to deride?

Of what avail the scholar's cultured thought;—
The artist's skill to fine perfection brought,
If all the beauty that their gifts have wrought,
    May come to naught?

Of what avail the maiden's dream of hope,
Cast in the light of Love's bright horoscope,
If she be left with powers beyond her scope,
    Alone to cope?

Of what avail? when every passing day
Takes with a cruel hand some friend away,
Whom we could earnest wish might ever stay
    To cheer our way.

Of what avail! Mysterious refrain;
The heart may echo o'er and o'er again,
But never quite this mystery explain
    To human ken.

We cry "of what avail," because we must;
We stand in doubting, even while we trust,
Yet somehow feel that to His child of dust
    God will be just.

Vain Glory.

I—CORINTHIANS X—12.

I gloried in my strength,
And never dreamed that my poor human will
Could weaken in its mastery of ill
    And yield the fight at length:

    And men, I knew, were blind;
But I, poor fool, presumed with impious thought,
That I of some diviner clay was wrought,
    With gifts above my kind.

    And so I dared my fate,
And placed no barrier in the tempter's way,
To keep my stumbling feet from going astray,
    Till came an hour too late:

    An hour of conscious sin;
When the sick heart would fain its errors cease,
In piteous longing for an hour of peace
    To quell the storm within.

    O! ye conceited souls,
Who proudly boast of an all conquering power
To stem Life's current in that fearful hour
    When madly swift it rolls.

    Your strength is but a boast,
And all your vaunted panoply of might
Availeth little on that dreadful night
    That finds you tempest-tossed.

Our World.

Our world seems very fair to Fortune's few;
   But there are struggling souls on every side
   At whom Existence seems but to deride
With subtle pictures of deceptive hue.
Upon the title page of Youth's fair morn
   Is read Hope's promise of a flattering tale,
A promise, but alas, too often born
   Of fantasies that fade and lights that pale.
As some bright sunrise all aglow with cheer,
   Melts into shadow, gathering mist and gloom,
So do Life's morning visions disappear,
   Lost in the clouds of unrelenting doom.
The World is fair, but all too sadly true,—
It seemeth fair but to a favored few.

Deal gently then, O ye of happier lot,
   With those whose sun has set in hopeless night;
   Fill with your cheery voice and presence bright,
Each sadly-silent, sorrow-darkened spot.
The world to some is very hard indeed;
   Even so hard that they have bowed the head,
   And craved the blissful quiet of the dead
To still the griefs that caused their hearts to bleed.
Yet they, as we, live by divinest right;
   For them, no less than us, are Earth's fair flowers;
But that a fickle fortune chose to blight
   The buds that decked the Spring-time of their hours.
Be such the kindly guise we daily wear,
That all the world shall seem to all most fair.

Christmas Rhymes.

1—Christmas Musings.
2—Christmas Greeting.
3—Christmas Remembrance.
4—Christmas Bells.

CHRISTMAS MUSINGS.

What cheer shall my Holiday greeting unfold
    For the welcome of those that are dear?
Shall I echo the fond Merry Christmas of old,—
For its castles in Spain with their treasures of gold,
And for happiness more than a life-time could hold,
    That might almost bring Paradise near?

Shall I ring out the changes which retrospect brings
    From the slumbers of far-away Youth,—
Shall I startle the dreams to which Memory clings,
While I summon the beautiful beings with wings
Who shall chant the quaint ballads that Santa-Claus sings,
    Till they glow with the beauty of Truth?

Ah! those castles in Spain; would they rise at my call,
    Though it sprang from my heart's fondest thought;
Farewell—such illusions—forever and all;
For Hope's proudest structures will crumble and fall
And leave but a desolate ruin of wall
    That will shelter but little or naught.

Idle fancies, perhaps—these weak wishes of mine;
    Almost seeming to mock and to jeer:
And I sometimes must think as I scan through the line,
So empty in fact though it read ne'er so fine,
That greetings like these hold more shadow than shine,
    And darken much more than they cheer.

Yet true hearts throb in tune with the holiday chimes,
    And the spirit grows blithesome and clear,
While the soul in such seasons has glimpses at times
Of the sunniest visions from Orient climes,
And the color of Hope tints my lack-a-day rhymes
    With an ardor both warm and sincere.

There are blessings that ride on the wings of intent,
    That will perfume the air as they fly;
And though ne'er may develop the wish that was sent,
Yet I fancy it carried sweet rest as it went,
And increased the world's measure of joy and content,
    With a richness that wealth cannot buy.

And I cherish the fiction that childhood has taught,
    As a charm that is real and true;
And I wish the old wishes of juvenile thought,
With their visions of hope and of happiness fraught,
With an added desire from experience bought,
    That they somehow may blossom anew.

Then I voice you again the old cheer, if you please,
    That my holiday musings inspire,
With a hope that the blessings of Life, (and in these
I include all the luck that good-fortune decrees,)
May surround you and yours with a comfort and ease
    That the happiest heart could desire.

Christmas Greeting.

May all the joys of Christmas-tide be thine
Upon this festal day, O friend of mine ;—
    May sunny smiles be thine the livelong day ;
        And lightened heart
        A charm impart
    To turn aside the shadows from the way.

Banish this day all tiring toil and care ;
Forget Life's crosses with their weary wear ;—
    Remember only the kind promise given
        That far-off day,
        In land away,
    Of the bright dream which pictures to us Heaven.

For "Peace on Earth" can only be complete
When human hearts find rest serene and sweet,
    And human love its loftiest height has reached,
        And not till then
        "Good will to men"
    May bear the fruitage long-for hoped and preached.

And in our quiet thought and clearer mood,
With Life's true lessons better understood,
    The Christmas teaching hints the happier way :
        So let us strive
        To keep alive
    The sweet and tender joys of Christmas Day.

Accept my greeting then, O friend of mine;
May all the joys of Christmas-tide be thine:—
   The Wealth of health, and friends and bounteous cheer;
     And rich increase
     Of Hope and Peace,
Make glad each moment of the coming year.

CHRISTMAS REMEMBRANCE.

Bathed in the sunshine of perennial youth
   And brightening all her pathway with her smile,
My friend exemplifies the welcome truth
   That angels have not quite gone out of style.
The march of Time, with more than usual grace,
   Has kindly passed this cheerful woman by;
Her years are not recorded in her face
   And brightly beams the twinkle in her eye.

And on this Christmas as I count my friends—
   Fewer, alas, with Time's incessant wear,
My thought goes out to one whose greeting lends
   An inspiration to an hour of care.
Long may the gladness of her life flow on,
   And green her memory last through all the years,
Whose cheerful presence bids dull care begone
   And from whose heart is born more smiles than tears.

CHRISTMAS BELLS.

Ah! yes, I hear them
Ringing in many ears with tones of gladness;
I also hear the piteous moans of sadness
    That echo near them.

Not all the pealing
Of steepled bells in merriest music chiming,
Nor Christmas carols e'er so gaily rhyming
    Can still the feeling,

That in Life's battle,
God's children lead forlornest hopes in sorrow,
With hearts that have no thought on Christmas morrow,
    For toy or rattle.

Too sadly often
There lurks a bitter grief or disappointment,
Some heartache that no healing wine or ointment
    Can soothe or soften;

And how can greeting
Come to a soul like this except in mocking—
When human ills and griefs are constant knocking
    With angry beating?

Yet Life can brighten,
And Hope in many a weary heart shall linger,
If but the gentle touch of friendly finger
　　Its load shall lighten;

　　And there come voices—
Even no more than Christmas carols singing,
Whose merry chimes in cheery echoes ringing,
　　Some heart rejoices.

　　Then ring your measure,
For longing ears may catch the sound and listen,
And sorrow-moistened eyes perchance may glisten
　　With tears of pleasure.

　　Ring out your story—
"Glory to God on High"—revere none other,
Let "Peace on earth and good will to our brother"
　　Fulfil His glory.

Memorial Tributes.

To John H. Galligan.

Suggested by reading one of his poems.

Not for one brief moment only rang the measure of his lay,
But the echoes of the minstrel's song are in our thoughts to-day,
And we catch the sober tenderness that rambles through his strain,—
All the more and sadly tender—his last lingering refrain.

And we scan again the picture that his artist fancy drew,
And we trace the joyous moments as he lived his childhood through,
And the youth who gave fair promise of a fairer yet to be
When the growth of soberer manhood cut the earlier tendrils free,—

And "those ripened days of manhood, rich and full with varied lore,"
Gilded bright with gorgeous color in the clustering fruit they bore,
As the promised wealth of boyhood found fulfilment strong and true
In a host of welcome virtues, blossoming each day anew.

Loyally thy friends have loved thee, with a loyalty of pride,
Proudly boasted of thy charity as generous and wide;
Told thy praises with a tireless zeal, and with no flattering tongue,
But tone of true sincerity, thy rich endowments sung.

But sad irony of Destiny, which blights with ruthless
    touch,
Fondest hopes that dwell so bright in thought, and
    promise us so much,
How the strength of sturdiest manhood melts in thy
    relentless grasp
And the bands, howe'er so strongly locked with earthly
    ties, unclasp.

Ah, that "Destiny that shapes our ends, rough hew them
    as we will,"—
Who can say the lot it brings to man shall work for good
    or ill?
While the fate that seemed so cruel to the ken of earthly
    eyes
May, through a diviner vision, prove an angel in disguise.

Spared our friend the withering wear of woes that four-
    score years might bring;
Spared the sad and painful retrospect that Winter gleans
    from Spring;
Spared the whitened locks, the drooping head, the loneli-
    ness of years,
And in their stead youth's heritage of friendship bathed
    in tears.

Poets chant of ripe old age and all the honor which it
    brings,
But my reason often questions if the poet rightly sings;
For the years bring added conflicts, leaving ugly scars
    of strife,
Which our love would gladly banish from the story of a
    life.

To an Honored Citizen.—B. W.

A kind and worthy man has dropped to rest,
   Who served his God in truest Christian way;—
   Not often opening wide his lips to pray,
But hourly giving to the world his best.
Through all the years almost beyond recall,
   Walked he in quiet way his Duty's round,
Nor swerved to right or left at any call
   Whose tones were false or of uncertain sound.
How little known and still less understood—
   A heart that kindles slow with friendly fire,
Because forsooth an unimpassioned mood
   Had been a birthright from a distant sire!
And thou—O silent friend—in life almost
   As silent as the space that bounds thee now;
There crowds upon our troubled thoughts a host
   Of Christian deeds, though lacking Christian vow.
"Well done, thou good and faithful one"—is thine;—
   A heritage for those whose hearts may bleed;
Nor towering stone nor epitaph so fine
   Can speak so well the comfort that we need.
Peaceful thy sleep must be whose many days
So little jostled with the world's rough ways.

A Friendly and Official Tribute at City Hall.—

Hon. H. L. C.

"An honest man's the noblest work of God;"
   Thus runs my thought, nor do I feel inclined
To seek expression of a loftier kind,
To praise the friend now resting 'neath the sod,
'Twould ill become one who has known him well,
   To deck with fulsome flattery his grave;
When simple mention of his name should tell
   In quick response, the compliments we crave.
A manly, open hand, that never failed
   To grasp its duty, be it stern or mild;
A stout, courageous heart that never quailed,
   And yet, withal, as tender as a child.
He was my friend—this man, and I may dare
   To say to others—strangers, it may be,—
That there are many we could better spare,
   And few, alas, from weaknesses more free.
Scan through his record made within these walls,—
   True to an oath not for one hour forgot,
And eye of keenest searching never falls
   Upon a page or line that marks a blot.
Remembering him whose life has passed away,
   And saddened by the thoughts that memories lend,
Than this, no higher tribute can I pay—
   "A just official, citizen and friend."

To a Wife and Mother.

Ended the day dreams born of hoped for joys;
　Sundered beyond restore Life's fairest plan;
Only fond memories left to guard her boys
　And lift the shadows from a lonely man.

I may not trust my feeble line to speak
　The boon of comfort that the heart most needs;
Language is mockery and all too weak
　To heal the wound that so profusely bleeds.
But I may give a word of earnest praise,
　Perchance to temper sorrow's cup with pride,
And make less grievous in the coming days,
　The saddened thoughts that linger and abide.
It seems a cruel hand that reaches out
　To quench the brightness of a happy home;—
Goodness Divine seems almost turned about,
　As seeking in unlovely paths to roam.
If there be any who should wear the crown,
　O wife and mother who have served your due,
When you have laid your weary burden down,
　Surely the richest meed should come to you.
They cannot hold her memory too dear,
　For whom her love and life were freely given,
And dreams of Heaven more real are and near,
　Since she has passed from sunlight into even.

We scatter flowers upon the grassy mound
   That only hides from sight a lifeless form,
As if we somehow thus had placed around
   A sheltering blessing from the blast and storm;
But if the closed and silent lips could speak,
   How slight the faith one needs but to believe
That she who rests beneath the daisies meek
   Would beg your loving thought for those that grieve.
O friends of those who mourn, be very kind,
   O sympathizing heart, give of your best;
The greatest boon humanity shall find,
   Is needed as its dear ones drop to rest.

"To rest"—Ah, yes;—Be grateful for the thought,
   A victory gained at last with cruel odds;
Weak from the standard of earth's battles fought;—
   Strong in her soul's approval and her God's.

To an Old Schoolmate.

Old friend, though I have not looked on thy face
    For many a year, yet I may not forget
That through thy boyhood I can easy trace
    The lines wherein our youthful friendships met.
I mind me not the cruel tales they told
    Of mis-spent hours and manhood's wasted prime,
The dross I saw not—but I knew the gold
    Of honest boyhood in the olden time.
And if when sterner fights of manhood pressed
    With heavy weight, they dragged thy foot-steps down,
'Tis not for me to pose in ease and rest
    And pass upon thy frailties with a frown.
I knew thee as a frank and generous lad,
    Whose heart was open and whose friendship true,
And clustering memories not unkind nor sad
    Have called to mind my boyhood's hours anew.

Thy voyage is over; 'tis the old, old tale—
    A fate-bound mortal on a storm-tossed sea;
And if some treacherous reef or blasting gale
    Shall end in wreck youth's fairest prophecy,
'Tis but the common lot of all, I ween—
Life's constant struggles with scant joys between;

And one by happy chance to-day may rise,
Yet on the morrow helplessly he lies.
As one may loftily his virtues boast,
Who—Heaven forgive him—needs forgiveness most,
While humble souls who little homage crave,
Have walked through life unnoticed, to the grave.
Thank Providence that in our final rest,
The meekest shares his chances with the best.

To an Old Schoolmate.—C. A. M.

Swift is the flight of Time! The years slip by;
   Youth's dearest comrades pass from thought and sight,
Till some brief printed line shall catch the eye
   And bring long-hidden memories to light.
How the old scenes come trooping through the brain;
   The youthful sports that made our sum of joys;
The roguish pranks revived and lived again,
   And thou, true friend, the prince among the boys.

In retrospect I hold thy memory dear,
   And more than formal tribute mayst thou claim;
For those who knew thee read a record clear
   And loved an honored and respected name.
Dear friend and schoolmate of the olden time,
   My boyish ideal of the strong and brave,
With sorrowing speech and sadly-halting rhyme,
   I plant this flower of friendship at thy grave.

Of a Friend and Classmate.

A cherished dream of Faith and Hope and Love!
A few brief years of earth's enjoyment given!
A sweet communion with her God above!
A saintly spirit upward flown to Heaven.

"A dream of faith;" aye, more than any dream;
  More clearly than through any fleeting vision,
Shone her sweet trust that made the Present seem
  But as a prelude to a world Elysian.

And patient "hopes" and dearest "loves;"—were these
  But only dreams that mocked in cruel scorning,
Or were they rather buds of glad hearts-ease,
  To bloom in fulness on the Heavenly morning?

E'en her sweet fancies wore the garb of Truth,
  So vividly shone forth each bright ideal,
And strengthened by the gladsome tone of Youth,
  Her Faith and Hope and Love were grandly real.

Her life was not a field of passions slain,
  Or daily combating with things contested;
Only the pure in heart could e'er attain
  Unto the heights on which her spirit rested.

Ye blinded souls who only look for saints
  Among the relics of the far-off ages,
This sweet, young life a finer picture paints,
  Than decks the records of your wisest sages.

And as the weary days and years pass on,
  And Time shall rest its shadowy gloom more lightly;
Shall bid the freshness of our grief be gone,
  And tinge the remnant of our life more brightly,

Dear, precious thoughts may come, though sad, yet sweet,
  Illumined by the light thou sheddest o'er them,
That, lovingly, may guard our halting feet
  From dangerous paths that ever lie before them.

And if the Christian hope proves not a dream,
  But finds fruition in a realm supernal,
Another world of Life shall brightly gleam
  With all the friendship of a Love eternal.

Farewell, dear friend! thou canst not but fare well,
  Whose life was such a brave and patient story,
Nor could the proudest record better tell
  The grand fulfilment of our Father's glory.

To the Memory of Private H. A. Williams, at a Reception given Battery F.

Halt for a moment in your hour of cheer:
Summon a comrade from the shadow-land:
Grant him a welcome at your banquet here
    And greet him with fraternal heart and hand.

He shared your crosses,—let him wear the Crown
    That well bedecks the martyrs' sainted roll,
And as you write your names of heroes down,
    Place his in golden letters on the scroll.

Count not the soldier fallen at his post,
    Less near or dear than those whom Fate has spared,
For who can reckon which deserveth most,
    Where those who lived or died alike have dared?

But as our plaudits fill your hearts with pride
    For task accomplished, and for duty done,
One moment lay your pleasantry aside
    For him whose earthly honors all are won.

And kindly pledge the absent one to-night
    Whose voice is sadly silent at your call,
A martyr to the loftiest dream of right,
    For he who gives his life has given all.

To the Local Philosopher.

What will the verdict be when we pass on?
   He must indeed be curiously wrought,
   Who never in his time has given thought
To what report might say when he is gone;—
Whether it blazon to the world his faults,
   Or, worse,—may damn with feeble, unearned praise,
Or if in love his memory exalts
   In kind regard for all his better ways.
Will men forgive our errors all these years,
   Which we, alas, have mourned not less than they,
And standing by our graves, plead with their tears
   That Life's unworthier part be hid away?
It may be little to the lifeless dust
   Whether they speak of us in praise or blame;
Yet who so base, that would not rather trust
   Virtue than vices, to protect his name.
Let those who write our epitaph but tell
Only the work that we accomplished well,
And for the ken of those who knew us not,
Something like this upon our tombstone jot—

"Here lies our Local Phil., who at its best,
Found his poor lot a wearisome unrest;
Like all mortality denied a voice
To make of life or nothingness his choice,
He struck this sphere at Destiny's command,
A feeble traveler in a hostile land.
For there are some who drift upon this shore
That fatten on Life's coarse turmoil and roar;
So strongly armed and splendidly equipped,
The subtlest snares have never fouled or tripped;
Another finds his chief inheritance
The poverty of weakness and mischance,
And meeting Fortune as a bitter foe,
Will yield the contest scarcely with a blow.
The sleeper here, judging from all report,
Trained in the legions of the weaker sort;
In reading Fate, interpreting the worst,
He owned to being beaten from the first;
Then spare unkindly criticism, friend,
On one who did but little worth pretend;
Let not thy tongue in blame or censure wag,
That he hath tripped on many a treach'rous snag,
But rather wonder that he struggled through,
Keeping the brighter side so much in view,
And speak your best of this defenceless dust;
Take his poor memory in kindly trust;
Forgive, and if within your power, forget
The debts he paid in paying Nature's debt."

Ah! we do care for words of good or ill;
    We wear a stubborn front from day to day,
    Brushing with free and careless hand away,
The world's regard as if it were but *nil*.
But there shall come an hour, thou proudest one,
    When thou and pride alike are lying low;
And when thine earthly course is nearly run,
    Thou canst not answer sympathy with "No,"
But earnest reaching forth with helpless hands,
    All torn and bleeding in a hopeless strife,
Confess the need of sympathetic bands
    To tie the sundered ligaments of Life.
Be this the lesson that our verse shall teach—
That human love shall higher levels reach.

To an Old Musical Friend.—J. N.

Another old campaigner gone to rest;
   And though he blazoned not the roll of fame,
   Yet would that we might write against our name
This record from his life—"he did his best."
His work was builded better than he knew;
   Long years of tender memories defend
   The modest soldier, citizen and friend,
In all that makes a noble manhood true.
His work is done:—no more the martial beat
Which rang with truest measure through the street,
(A fitting echo to his generous heart,)
Shall old-time thoughts and memories impart.
Another hand than his has beat the roll
And placed our comrade on a new patrol.

Rhymes for the Occasion.

1—The Old School St. School.
2—At an Aldermanic Supper.
3—For a Golden Wedding.
4—At a Silver Wedding.
5—Memorial Day, 1884.
6—Memorial Day, 1894.
7—Dedication High School Building.
8—Taunton's 250th Anniversary.

THE OLD SCHOOL ST. SCHOOL.

"And then the whining school-boy," says the bard,
With satchel and with shining morning face,
Creeping like snail, unwillingly to school."
                —*Shakespeare's Seven Ages.*

Ah! well, perhaps 't were so in Shakespeare's day,
    When but a little learning did suffice
And ignorance was bliss in mocking guise,
While education loitered on the way:
It might have been when only royal rank
    Monopolized the learning of the land,
And when the peasant's poor ambition shrank
Beneath the pressure of a tyrant's hand—
When might was right, and liberty unknown,
    And human birthright was akin to Fate,
Enriching him who sat upon a throne,
    And bidding Fortune's humbler vassals wait,
Then might the boy, as sang the bard of yore,
    Creep like the snail unwillingly to school,
And little reck if well-earned laurels wore,
    Or perched the victim on a dunce's stool.

I speak the story of a kinder age,
   And ring the changes of a clearer chime;
With free and certain hand I turn the page
   That holds the record of a happier time.
No whining schoolboy greets my vision now;
   The shining morning face perchance I see,
But with a hopeful crown upon the brow
   That banishes the word "unwillingly."
The nineteenth-century village lad may mount
A higher pinnacle than duke or count;
The little lass who sits so primly there,
May in the years adorn the White House chair;
There is no limit to the mete or bound
That hedges earnest, honest worth around;
But these are homilies so often told,
That my poor verse no newer truths unfold,
And I may be excused for turning back
Just for one moment from the beaten track.

A picture moves before me from the Past,
That seems to hold its colors strong and fast—
A sketch from real life which marks the plot
That represents the average human lot,
And could I show these girls and boys to-day,
Wherein their feet may walk on Life's highway;
What heights they may attain by earnest toil,
Or by neglect their youth's fair promise spoil;
If I might hope some courage to inspire,
And lift their youthful aspirations higher,
This simple picture offered to your view
Is proof of what the years may bring to you;

For all too quick must come your hour of care,
And school-day life is gone ere you're aware:
"So soon the boy a youth, the youth a man,
Eager to run the race his father ran."
Well for the youth if he shall win the race
Unsullied by dishonor and disgrace ;
And this my picture shows a record fair
Within the reach of every one to share.

And, first, the school-boy—not the whining youth
That Shakespeare sends us down in garb uncouth,
But brimming full with all the life and joy
Which mark your healthy, happy, ideal boy;
With just enough of mischief in his mix
To perpetrate the latest school-boy tricks.
For his few faults let charity be broad ;
A perfect boy is apt to prove a fraud.
And this was one, it cannot be denied,
Whose failings largely leaned to Virtue's side.
This youth, as gathered from the old reports,
Excelled in all the boyish games and sports ;
His quest for pleasure was a genuine one,
And gave an air of business to the fun ;
His fishing trips, as told in idle while,
Would make the dullest-minded listener smile;
His love of ball has never died away,
And he'd go miles to see a game to-day ;
While often do I hear my friend recite
His boyish escapades with keen delight,
Developing this fact in nature's plan—
The manly youth lives as a youthful man.

But hold, and let a few years intervene,
And lift the curtain on another scene;
The boy has said "Good Bye" to book and slate
And in the mart of business chanced his fate :—
A Main street merchant, with an eye for gain,
With ample capital—of pluck and brain :—
Whose days of toil were arduous and long
And labor formed the burden of his song.
Now comes the application of some rule
That so perplexed his faculties at school;
The old arithmetic, despised at times,
Now aids to add and multiply his dimes,
And he discovers—what before unknown,
That Education is the poor man's throne.

But comes the sound of war—this boy had fought
The mimic warfare of an urchin's thought;
Had charged with reckless bravery the camp,
Within which lay entrenched some youthful scamp;
In paper hat and armed with wooden gun,
Had vanquished infant foemen, one by one;
And, Alexander-like, had vainly sighed
Because earth's battlefields were not more wide.
Smile, if you will, at childish pastime spent
In mock parade and burlesque armament;
Laugh at the boy who finds his keenest sport
Behind the ramparts of a snow-clad fort,
But read the story of your School street boys
Who played at warfare and whose guns were toys,
And then your country's list of heroes scan,
Who heard the war-cry and who led the van,

Then lay your unkind thought or sneer away,
And save your laughter for another day :
For here sat heroes of the truest stamp,
Heard from in every battlefield and camp,
And foremost, Freedom's banner to defend,
We find our school-boy and our merchant friend.
The tale, for lack of time, must be made brief,
And rapid turn we each successive leaf :
How well the soldier battled for the truth,
And justified the promise of his youth,
With real sword and gun how bravely fought
In mightier war than school-day history taught;
How, wounded and a prisoner, he bore
The heaviest burden that a patriot wore ;
And how, with shattered health and wearied form,
No longer fit to face the battle storm,
He turned reluctant from the field of strife,
And won the honors of a civic life,
Is blazoned in a history that would shame
The old time conqueror for power and fame.
His record is our pride—it should be yours—
An aid when baser influence allures—
A living lesson that shall fairly teach
What honors lie within a willing reach,
For he was one of many that we know
Who filled these benches not so long ago;
I only sketch this lad from out the rest
Because I chance to know his history best,
And (I may say it with a proper pride)
Because of friendship long and truly tried.

A word for one whose loved and absent face
Has left a sacred memory in this place,—
The dear old teacher of that earlier day,
Whose mortal form has just been laid away.
Kindest of men, he lingers in my thought
As one whose love transcended what he taught.
In those old times when flogging ruled the hour
And muscle more than knowledge far was power,—
When teachers thought their day's work not performed
Unless a dozen jackets they had warmed,
His kindly love his sense of justice swerved
And never gave us half that we deserved.
Peace to the record of so many years
That leaves no cause for grief, no room for tears,
Only the sad regret when all is past,
That lives so true cannot forever last.

Grave shadows flit within these walls to-day;
   At Memory's call I see the little world
Wherein my youthful banners were unfurled
In many a briskly-fought scholastic fray:
Long years have passed since I, a careless lad,
   Answered the roll-call from this very floor,
Sat at these desks, made record good or bad,
   And longed for what the Future held in store:
It seems so like a dream—this backward look—
Back to the distant time of slate and book;
When care was yet unborn and Life all hope,
Seen clear and bright through Youth's glad horoscope.
The eye may dim with years, but never blind
To visions of the past becomes the mind;

The constant din of daily life may dull
    The worn and weary ear to sounds of earth,
But none the less shall echo clear and full
    That far-off youthful revelry and mirth.
And not all reminiscences are sad;
'Tis only those that waken keen regret
For grievous errors we would fain forget,
Or as we think of Life's work unfulfilled,
Where Death some youthful heart and pulse has stilled,
That retrospect in sombre garb is clad:
But peeping through the memory-laden mists,
    Are sunny rifts of bright and joyous hue,
    As childhood's hours are reproduced anew,
    And quaint remembrances of bygone days,
    Of sundry curious boyish pranks and plays
Remind us that our boyhood still exists.
Cherish those thoughts of childhood, girl and boy;
    Cling to the airy castles of your youth;
Let not the wear and tear of life destroy
    Your earlier dreams of innocence and truth,
For age in waning years turns back to these,
    With longing look and with a hungry heart,
And counts its comforts as the glance may please,
    Of scenes wherein we bore an honored part.

At an Aldermanic Supper.

ON RETIRING FROM OFFICE.

There preached a parson in the olden time,
Who fondly hoped to glean a vagrant dime,
When preacher's salaries did not wax fat,
By passing 'round among his flock, his hat:
He labored zealously one Sabbath through,
As old-time ministers were wont to do,
Warmed to the task with an unusual fire,
To prove the "laborer worthy of his hire."
Somehow or other his remarks fell cold
And failed to have a grip upon the fold,
And for some reason which is unexplained
His plea for recompense was not sustained.
The sermon done, round went the parson's tile
In expectation of a generous pile,
But states the tale—"the hat, we grieve to say,
Returned as empty as it went away."
The saddened preacher with despondent mien,
Took in the disappointment of the scene;
Then as all well-bred Christian teachers ought,
Found comfort in a last relieving thought;—

"For joys prospective, he but little cared;
Sufficient unto him the blessing spared;"
And so with grateful heart and tone devout,
His prayer of Christian thankfulness went out
As on his graceless flock his glance was cast—
"Thank God, I have my beaver back at last."

My Aldermanic service through, I find
This old-time incident brought back to mind;
Like the poor preacher have I had my day
Of thankless service and of doubtful pay;
Like him I too have passed the hat around
Hoping for some approving word or sound,
And like his, also, was response so rare,
It must have died upon the empty air;
But yet like him I have a solace left,
From which in no way can I be bereft;—
For what I failed to get I'll not repine;
For what is spared me, gratitude be mine;
No more I stand in dread of critic sneers
From which I vainly strive to close my ears;
No more am I compelled with stumbling feet
To locate Dean Street Bridge or Scadding Street;
Nor 'mid confusing claims, beset to mark
The best location for a Public Park;
The wooden structure and the hitching post;
The taxes, sewers, street lights, and a host
Of other vexing questions, pro and con,
Which city fathers needs must pass upon;
With some of which old Solon might have failed,
And famed Lycurgus in his best days paled;

Whose knotted mazes we have struggled through,
To learn, alas, how little each one knew.
Never again shall license question serve
To test the strength of Aldermanic nerve ;
Cursed, not alone by those who buy and sell,
But damned by Prohibitionist as well—
A paradox for some one to define,
Whose brain is more circuituous than mine ;—
These all are phantoms now at which I smile,
And wonder why I dreaded them the while ;
Content am I in private life, to wave
A flag of truce above their peaceful grave,
Where, by the grace of Heaven, may they stay
Until the final trump of Judgment Day,
When every Alderman shall have his due
In high-toned glory or sulphuric blue.
As the poor preacher with spasmodic glee,
Snatched from defeat a gleam of victory,
And in a heaven-born philosophic mood
Could recognize none other than the good,
So I, though shorn of my official power,
Look only at the vantage of the hour,
And shout with more of pleasure than of pain—
"Thank Heaven! I have my freedom back again."

For a Golden Wedding.

My dear young friends of fifty wedded years;—
  So young that we can scarce believe the tale:
Old age with gathering shadows disappears
    And in your sunlight youthful thoughts prevail.
The frosts of Time have little power to chill
    The sunny smiles that rest upon your brow,
And you can mount the summit of Life's hill
    With glad remembrance of your youthful vow.
We speak of angels, and the skeptics scoff,
    As if such curious creatures could not be,
Or, at the best they live perchance, far off,
    With wings and halos mortals never see:
But I may banish angels from my thought,
    So long, dear friends, as I may think of you:
The pictures drawn by preacher never taught
    Of human lives more faithful or more true.
Long may you cheer us with your happy guise
    So graceful worn and with such sweet content,
And may the friends you cherish duly prize
    The kindly blessing which your love has sent.

AT A SILVER WEDDING.

After the Parson, in descending rank,
At times like this, comes the poetic crank :—
A grievous tumble from the heights sublime,
From preacher's eloquence to huckster's rhyme ;
And yet the philosophic view of ill,
Which finds a virtue in the weakest pill,
And which, whenever rightly understood,
Evokes from every form of evil, good,
Presents a strong hypothesis to back it ;
Which starts me on a little story racket.

An ancient darkey, (so the story ran,)
Struck out for pleasure on a novel plan,
And like a monk doing penance for his sins,
Sat by the roadside, pommeling his shins.
Now all men whether college-bred or not,
Know of a colored brother's tender spot,
And why this ancient gent in native black,
Should wantonly his tender organs whack,
Was quite a puzzle to the passers by,
Who watched the sufferer with a curious eye,
Till one kind soul with sympathetic bump,
Whose heart endured a pang with every thump,

Advanced a small conundrum as a starter:
"What was the need to pose as such a martyr?"
The sable brother with a radiant smile,
Betokening Heaven-born comfort all the while,
Although forsooth, his inward stress of soul
Revealed his fitness for St. Stephen's role,
Threw out a new philosophy of pain,
Which showed he had not lived and learned in vain;—
The soothing joy when pain was over, brought
Full compensation for the suffering wrought;
To use an explanation of his making,—
"It done feel better when it get through aching."
And here the moral of our story fits;—
All I can offer from my scattering wits,
As any contribution to your fun,
Is the relief you'll feel when I am done.

But friends, I take a measure of delight
In speaking up my little piece to-night;
It's very seldom that I have a chance,
Where every point of fact and circumstance
Permits a chap to say so much that's good,
And not mix in some taffy with the food.
When one so many years has played his part
A well known figure in the public mart,—
Never at any time, so far as heard,
Unworthy either in his act or word;
And in his record nothing can offend,
Either as soldier, citizen or friend;
Who, when a charity is talked about,
Offers to turn his pockets inside out;

Has always paid his honest debts in full,
And never palmed off shoddy for all-wool;
Who pays his pew-tax promptly at the call,
And sleeps through service little, if at all;
And when the deacons pass the box in church,
Loans me a quarter if I'm in the lurch;
Who never had to be kept after school
Because he hadn't learnèd the Golden Rule;
And, though he lay his Bible on the shelf,
Shows up the Ten Commandments in himself;
A man exemplifying chronic good,
Who can't act mean, and wouldn't if he could;
Who always keeps his cheerful side in sight,—
This is the man we're showing up to-night.

Now as the press would say, a paragraph
With some allusion to the other half.
Not posing quite as plainly as a mark,
I may be shooting somewhat in the dark,
Yet all the logic of fair play infers
That half the credit of the house is hers;
The wife who well and ably fills her sphere
Till wedlock scores its five and twentieth year,
Has proved that when her husband picked her out
He knew quite certain what he was about:
That she has played domestic partner well,
Speaks for itself better than I can tell;
That she has kept her friendships warm and bright,
Is advertised upon the cards to-night;
That she has faithfully performed the part
Required of her in culinary art,

Will scarcely be denied, if you will note
The growing fulness of her husband's coat.
No Benedict is quite the perfect man
With home a circus or a caravan;
Nor can he long a cheerful mood retain
With Caudle lectures ringing in his brain,
And the true measure of a husband's cares
Is often indexed by the face he wears.

All honor to our worthy host to-night,
Honors are his by every well-earned right;
The honors of a true man born and bred;
Honors of kindly heart and level head;
The honors of a life of many years,
Whose record calls for no regretful tears;
Honors and blessings;—blessing of this home,
With happiest welcome to the guests who come;
Blessed with a wife, enjoying by his side,
The fullest measure of a wifely pride,
Who, when the roll of husbands has its call,
Counts hers the "noblest Roman of them all."
Who dares and has the right to think her spouse
The equal of the head of any house;
And though in introducing household joys,
By some mistake they counted out the boys,
One crowning blessing, dutiful and fair,
Reflects the virtues of the worthy pair.

May it be long before the shadows come
To cloud the brightness of this pleasant home,
And as the fleeting years of Time go by,
May blessings, love and honor multiply.

MEMORIAL DAY, 1884.

READ AT THE SERVICES OF POST 3, G. A. R.

A day of memories of a sacred past!
A day of memories crowding close and fast,
Waking, in echoes of a distant strife,
Our too-forgetful reverence to life.
How little can a man of peaceful mood,
Who never in the front of battle stood;
Whose ear was not attuned to martial note
Nor listened to the cannon's brazen throat;
Who earned no laurels in those troublous days,
Save such as crown the Quaker's quiet ways,
And used, in conflict with his fellow men,
No keener weapon than a halting pen;—
How feebly can such voices ring the chimes
That wake the echoes of those stirring times,
Where men have proved, through valiant heart and might
Their claim as heroes, by divinest right?
How can they call up legends of the camp—
The weary march and wearier midnight tramp;
The gallant picket at his lonely post;
The watchful sentry like some spectral ghost
Or restless spirit, stalking to and fro—
A constant menace to a treacherous foe?
These to civilians are historic dreams;
How can they build them into living themes,
Painting a picture in their fancy's glow,—
A faithful copy of that long ago?
Who can call up in visions that are clear,
Those mem'ries distant and yet ever near,

Save him, the record of whose warlike days
Sets all the fires of memory ablaze?
For those who scent the battle from afar,
Scarce grasp "the pomp and circumstance of war,"
"He jests at scars who never felt a wound,"
And little comprehends of sacred ground,
Whereon his recreant feet have never trod
In service of his country or his God.

Life rings new changes in its circling round;
The march of Time knows neither mete nor bound:
A reign of Peace has banished with its spell,
The sadder sounds of War's funereal knell.
Yet glow those scenes as vividly to-day,
As if the years had never passed away.
Sad be that hour and dull that comrade's soul,
Which answers not responsive to the roll;
Which can forget, in Life's engrossing care,
The laurels that the hero's brow should wear;
And of all nobler impulse losing hold,
Measures existence by its weight in gold.
Not such the fame for which the patriot strives,
As worth its recompense in human lives,
But prizing, with a fond and sacred pride,
His love of country over all beside.

It needs no lofty monument to tell
How these, her children, served their country well,
Nor can a marble tablet best express
The record of a martyr's faithfulness.
The little banner that so meekly waves
In mute memorial beside their graves,

Speaks to the heart in truer, tenderer tones,
Than pile on pile of monumental stones.
God has implanted in the human breast,
A sense of worship far more fitly drest
In the sweet homage of a simple flower,
Than stately granite blocks that Heavenward tower;
For these, instead of trumpeting renown,
May only press the dust of cowards down.

In coming years a traveler's feet may stray
Where we have lain our precious dead away;
Perchance with curious thought will halt beside
Two mounds of earth that nestle side by side;
And from the head of one shall upward climb
Like some huge obelisk of ancient time,
A giant shaft, that in its height, would aim
To link in Heaven with its owner's name.
Yet all this vain display and mock parade—
A hero worship born of Mammon's aid,
But little indicates the real worth
Which finds a shelter 'neath this mound of earth,—
The record of whose tenant, truly told,
But hollow, selfish echoes of his gold;
Only the poor apology for one .
Who in his time, less good than ill had done.

But near this grandly decorated mound,
The stranger's eye shall fall on lowlier gound,
All unadorned except with Nature's grace;—
No stone to mark its owner's resting place;
Naught but a faded wreath of immortelle
And the dear banner that he loved so well,

Shall tell the traveler that the buried dust
Is the fond relic of a nation's trust;
Yet, in the verdure of immortal bloom,
The sleeping tenant of that humbler tomb,
Shall need no pleading voice to urge the claim
That lifts his memory to perennial fame.

These are our heroes that we reverence here;
For them we hold such sad memorials dear;
Backward a score of years we turn our thought
To martial glories and to battles fought;
Again a warlike din our senses greets;
The soldier's tramp is ringing through the streets:
"Grim-visaged War" is shadowing peaceful life
And all the air is redolent of strife.
Again we bid farewell with moistened eye
To those who march to Death or Victory;
Once more from every hearthstone in the North,
The earnest prayers of loyal hearts go forth;
Prayers for the weal of those we hold most dear;
Prayers that the murky air of war might clear,
Bringing, with all that peace and quiet lends,
A host of heroes to their hosts of friends.
These are not dreams but visions all too true,
Which sad and stern realities renew;
That tell a tale of grand heroic worth,
Protecting Freedom in its right of birth;
Teaching the world that with each passing year,
Not less does human liberty grow dear,
And every age in every coming reign,
Shall bring its heroes to the front again.

Memorial Day, 1894.

THE LAST COMRADE.

March your proudest, honored patriot, while your step is
 firm and strong;
Shout your loudest, valiant soldier, as your voice peals
 out in song;
Sound your glory with the echoes of the trumpet and the
 drum,
That the story may be ringing through the centuries to
 come.

Loyal hearts are warmly throbbing to the music of your
 tramp;
Memory starts the songs and legends of the bivouac and
 camp;
Almost seems the scene repeated, were it not that while
 we gaze,
Waking dreams of faltering footsteps cloud the light of
 other days.

Joy and pleasure wed with sadness in this springtime of
 the year,
And a measure born of gladness, kindly mingles with
 your tear,
And you lighten sorrow's burden in these sadly-sacred
 hours,
As you brighten with your tribute of the season's fairest
 flowers.

But the ages mock at memory, and the time is all too
    near,
When the pages of your hero-life must dim and dis-
    appear,
And your column, strong and stately though it marches
    forth to-day,
Tells in solemn notes of warning that its strength must
    wear away.

Time is lending with stern usury the days that fly too
    fast;
Backs are bending with a burden that must weigh them
    down at last;
Ranks are thinning while no fresh recruits can swell your
    gallant band;
Death is winning slowly, surely, every fight with certain
    hand.

Have you never, valiant soldier, as you decked those
    graves in May,
Thought that ever in the future there must come a
    fateful day,
When some lonely, weary veteran, last survivor of his
    Post,
Must the only remnant linger of a vast and mighty
    host?

Have you pondered which among you last should lay
    his burden down?
Have you wondered whose the weary brow to wear this
    martyr's crown—
Who the tired, tottering one shall be, the last sad tale
    to tell,
Uninspired by any sight or sound of those he loved so
    well?

As romances create heroes, with imagination free,
In my fancies I have pictured whose this pilgrim-form might be;
Lifelike, truthful, bright before me, as a portrait from the sun,
Stands a youthful, boyish volunteer of Eighteen Sixty-one.

Just a lad when he enlisted, able scarce his gun to bear.
But enclad in knightly spirit, such as manliest heroes wear;
And ye err, who in your careless thought speak slightingly of youth,
Which may stir with glowing ardor on the side of God and Truth.

But the boys are boys no longer; youth is manhood,— manhood, age,
And the joys of youth have ripened to the wisdom of the sage,
And though real yet Life's battle, pressing constant, close and fast,
Not less leal is the soldier to his memories of the past.

How the faces of his comrades must to him grow doubly dear,
As he traces by their footsteps, passing mile stones, year by year,
And what clustering emotions must be struggling in his soul,
As the mustering-out commander drops another from the roll.

One step nearer to the last, he thinks;—one nearer to
    the end;
Each one dearer that is spared him now, and closer as a
    friend,
And his aching heart rebels at every summons of the
    Hand
That is taking surely, one by one, the remnant of his
    band.

There must come a halt ere long, brave youth; ah! youth
    no longer now;
"Nearer home," with every passing May, is traced upon
    thy brow,
And each season that the march of Time is written on
    Life's page
Stamps as treason youth's brave contest in its battling
    with Age.

But within my fancy's vision, at no far-off distant day,
With the din of conflict lost in space and hushed all
    hostile fray.
On some May Memorial morning shall our soldier boy of
    yore
Plod his way in painful solitude for aye and evermore.

Not again his lot to decorate the graves of gallant men;
Quite in vain the strength, says Holy Writ, of four score
    years and ten.
And it needs no voice prophetic to remind the valiant
    soul
That his deeds henceforth can have no speech except on
    Memory's scroll.

Time has banished with a cruel hand the lightness of his
    tread;
And the vanished power of manhood's pride is slumber-
    ing and dead,
And the graves where sleep his comrades, move him
    sadly as he sees
How the braves have fallen round him like the leaves
    from off the trees.

Stilled the clamor and the turmoil of those ancient days
    afar;
Gone the glamour of the trappings and the pageantry of
    war;
Pomp and splendor pass unnoticed, relics of a bygone
    age;
True and tender memories only mark the veteran's heri-
    tage.

Dreams of battles haunt his visions—always dreams of
    battles won,
And he prattles in derision as the foemen break and run;
Bloodless fields of retrospection constant crowd upon his
    brain
And he wields in thought, with waning strength, the
    ancient sword again.

Nurse thy dreaming, gallant soldier,—'tis the privilege
    of years,
That, in seeming, Age may wear again its earlier smiles
    and tears,
And the heat of battle kindles from the embers of
    decay,
As the beat of drum and martial note shall charm the
    years away.

Fare thee well, thou faithful sentinel upon thy lonely
    round!
Legends tell in song and story of the pilgrim's hallowed
    ground;
But my thought in farthest reaching pictures no more
    sacred shrine
Richer fraught with precious memories than this resting
    place of thine.

May the God of battles comfort thee, thou weary one
    and worn;
May the sod that rests above thee bloom with each
    Memorial morn,
And the waves of loyal gratitude, in never-ceasing tide,
Guard the graves of those we hold so dear with rever-
    ence and pride.

Dedication
High School Building.

"New times demand new measures and new men."
In fond remembrance of my schoolday ken,
I quote this fragment of an old-time verse,
So oft declaimed in better form or worse.
To-day, long years from far-off school-day age,
The schoolboy once more stands upon the stage;
And the old text which in his thoughtless youth,
Held in its shell an undeveloped truth,
In garb of newer colors, bright and warm,
Takes on its fuller and a better form.
These are "new times;" farewell for good or ill,
Those days whose vivid memories haunt us still;
Here also are "new measures;" who shall doubt
That newer plans will crowd the old ones out,
When all these fair surroundings plainly teach
The lesson more than eloquence of speech.
Here springs to life the cherished dream of years;
The oft-sown seed of mingled hopes and fears
Have, after many seasons, taken root,
And in this noble structure borne their fruit.
The prayers of youths and maidens in the past,
Have found their tardy answer here at last:
The prize of long endeavor has been won;
The perfect work of Patience bravely done.
And here, though not a pedagogue by rule,
Let me suggest a lesson for the school,—

The simple one of Patience, seldom learned
In time to have its better use discerned,—
An attribute of rare intrinsic worth,
As fundamental as the laws of earth,
By which the dullest scholar climbs to heights
Not always mastered in more rapid flights.
Thank Heaven for Patience! 'Tis a goodly gift,
And helps us many a wearying load to lift,
I know your text books skip it, yet I think
They give to weaker themes their space and ink.

But I forget; I was not asked to teach,
Nor make a long or dry pedantic speech.
The hour is one for joyousness and cheer,
And lighter lines are more in order here.
Suppose we throw the light on other scenes,
That seemed familiar to us in our teens,
And with a harmless, retrospective knife,
Dissect a section of our schoolday life;
Go back with me awhile and take a look
At where we struggled with the slate and book.

My memory may prove a little slow
With things that happened fifty years ago,
But somewhere near that time, beyond all doubt,
The primal high school hung its banner out;
Like Barnum's moral and instructive show,
Imparting information on the "go";
Halting at divers points about the town,
To polish our ambitious youngsters down.
It hardly seems in taste to criticise
The methods which our fathers reckoned wise,

Yet one can scarce repress a quiet smile
At thought of schooling in this novel style.
By whom conceived—this institute on wheels—
A kind and most considerate fate conceals,
And for his sake, whatever be his name,
We'll not disturb his somewhat doubtful fame.

But give the wheel of Time a few more whirls,
And interview our class of boys and girls;
For here we are at home and vouch for facts
No more in question than the Book of Acts.
Here was the high school that had come to stay;
The nucleus of this perfect plant to-day.
Survey a sketch of our old schoolday lot,
Drawn by our special artist on the spot:
Location, Spring street; on a grassy perch,
A grand old ruin of a worn-out church.
No longer fit for Christians, but preserved
As being quite as good as we deserved.
Its architecture, one might safe remark,
In many points bore semblance to the Ark;
Good ventilation (of a certain class,)
Maintained through sundry fractured lights of glass;
Only one stove to heat a boundless space;
(Comfort in school was ruled quite out of place).
A mile of rusty stovepipe, more or less,
Whose battered joints were pictures of distress;
And furniture (so styled in playful way,)
Would scandalize the junkshop of to-day.
This was our high school, and with tools like these,
Your charter members worked their first degrees;

And here was exercised the proud pursuit
Of teaching young ideas how to shoot.
"Poor chance for markmanship," perhaps you say,
But yet, my doubting friends, we blazed away,
And here record for those inclined to laugh,
That our old mill ground out more wheat than chaff.
Within those shaky walls were castles built,
That shone and dazzled with resplendent gilt.
Oft, by the aid of fancy's magic power,
We made our fortune in a single hour;
Not difficult just then, but yet a feat
Which, later on, not many could repeat.
There embryotic statesmen pulled the wires
Of juvenile political desires;
The young physician there his plans would nurse
To bleed the race in body and in purse;
Unconscious that where one his skill might save,
As many more he hurried to the grave.
Our would-be lawyers then had never dreamed
That Justice wasn't always what it seemed,
And that their greatest victories must be won
In efforts to prevent its being done;
Hence our attorneys, in their guileless youth,
Always defended Innocence and Truth,
A practice growing sadly out of vogue,
When almost every client proves a rogue,
And bribes so often stimulate the brief,
That lawyers thrive while Justice comes to grief.
Poets were more than scarce, as doth appear,
Else would your humble servant not be here,
A painful recollection of his time
Being a censure of his doggerel rhyme.

In every branch of science, trade and art,
Our little world of scholars had its part;
Each individual life a mimic plan
To mark the future of the coming man.

Now, looking at the picture we have drawn
Of our old high school in its early dawn,
One can't help being tempted to contrast
The value of the present with the past;
If in that worn-out antiquated shell,
We worked up scholars tolerably well,
So, by sound logic, here should graduate
Scholastic merit in its highest state.
May teachers find their efforts not in vain
To bring their labor to a higher plane;
Not high alone in theoretic form,
Some ornamental, classic height to storm,
But leading pupils on with less pretence,
On the broad basis of good common sense.
Your Greek and Latin and such things as these,
Buy little in the marts of bread and cheese,
And though man may not live by bread alone,
Without it he could scarcely hold his own.
Let not the cynic, in a sneering way,
Propound that school conundrum of to-day,—
"How far the scholar can be crammed for show,
To gild and hide the little he may know."
Somewhat sarcastic, but in measure true,
Where one is crowding too much study through.
These are but crude and homely hints from one
Who rates the worth of life by labor done;

Whose struggle with the Fates long since dispelled
All playful fancies that his schooldays held;
For life means business to the man of years,—
Often a gift of bitterness and tears,
Through which the weary worker seeks in vain
Some compensation for his toil and pain.
And it might come in hours like this, perchance,
Could some old memory or backward glance
But picture us again as girls and boys
And make us grateful for those earlier joys.
In hours of sober thought and solitude,
I wander through the past in reverent mood.
Bidding all present care awhile to go,
I walk again the paths I used to know.
The pictures of my boyhood greet my sight;
The sports and pranks of youth once more delight;
The dead past's ghosts have not been called in vain
And I am back with youthful friends again.
The sound of voices stilled with vanished years
Again in happiest cadence fills my ears;
Hands long since done with busy life, once more
Reach out in greeting as in days of yore.
Only a moment will the picture stay;
Before to-day's strong light soon fade away
Those dim and dusty memories that hold
So much, alas! that never can be told.
Ah, me! how everything has changed since then;
Girls are grave matrons and the boys staid men;
If that were all,—were cruel fate content
To spare the friends that Providence has lent,
E'en though its heavy hand of care had torn
Away the joyous look that youth had worn;

If this might be and that they had not died,
But lived with us and labored by our side,
Then added joys might be the sum of years
And smiles their heritage instead of tears.

Forgive me if I linger here too long,
But tides of memory run swift and strong,
And here, in freshly consecrated walls
Of new and brighter hopes, their shadow falls.
I would not dare its presence to ignore,
Nor pass its hallowing influence lightly o'er.
So much that helps to hold the future fast
Comes from the inspiration of the past,
That who omits this factor in the strife
Has not yet learned the rudiments of life.
May scholars of the future not despise
The steps by which their fathers sought to rise,
Nor fancy, with inordinate conceit,
That their success is sure to be complete.
For no school edifice, however grand,
Can create finished scholars at command;
"Fine feathers make fine birds," yet, none the less,
A bird may sweetly sing in plainer dress.
But in so far as scholarship depends
On all the aid that taste and beauty lends;
If comfort helps to lubricate the mind
And make its problems easier to unwind;
If with good ventilation, light and air,
Good health may also claim an added share;
Then are you blessed beyond your father's day,
With gifts which tax your utmost to repay,

Repay by earnest effort constant made;
By manhood of a higher, nobler grade;
By kindly thought and praise to others given,
Who, friendless and unhelped, have hopeless striven.
In poring over books do not forget
The graces in which character is set;
Instil the primal virtues in the mind;
Be not ungrateful, selfish nor unkind;
The world needs book-lore only as it lifts
The race from out desponding sloughs and drifts.
By such results your fathers shall be told
In what esteem their liberal gift you hold;
Let not the end for lack of effort made
Give rise to any thought of hope betrayed.

And now your bard an item would rehearse
To give a tone of moral to his verse:
When called upon to take this part to-day
He very promptly in his mind said, "Nay;
Some other one than I must fill the bill,
The task is one that's quite beyond my skill."
But, meeting with a friend whose level head,
When mine was weak, I've often used instead,
Was plainly told that no one ought to shirk
Even what seemed most uncongenial work.
I saw the point, was conquered, and I came;
If I have bored you, on him rests the blame;
And yet his reasoning was doubtless sound,—
"Wherever needed, be your service found."
No better lesson can the hour suggest;
Let duty solve all doubts and do your best.

250TH ANNIVERSARY

OF

SETTLEMENT OF TAUNTON.

A staunch old proverb in parental tone
Sagely remarks—"Let well enough alone;"
The tale is told—and fitly told; what need
That I, whose tribute must be weak indeed,
Should dim, by thoughts whose lightness might profane,
The charm these reminiscent hours contain?
But Fashion, with its many curious laws,
Writes in its code an after-dinner clause,
And this provides that though profuse the feast,
Yet shall the list of viands be increased
By adding superfluities thereto,
To tempt the pampered appetite anew;
Thus was I summoned to this bounteous spread,
Whose guests already have been overfed,
Upon the chance presumption—we will say—
That I might have some dainty stored away:
And as the Jester at the kingly court,
Must needs contribute to the festive sport,
Though airy chaff and jokes but feebly made,
May be, perchance, his only stock in trade,
So I, though neither king nor lord decree,
Will all too gladly seal my loyalty,

And, minus cap and bells, will forge and cast
My link to chain the Present with the Past.
Two centuries and a half have bottled up
The wine we pour to-day from memory's cup,
And who may censure if the overflow
Should swamp some champion's wit and lay him low?
What would your ideal Yankee be without
His proud prerogative to sing and shout?
Deal gently, then, with every awkward slip,
If, in exuberance, the Muse should trip,
And while it labors for the public weal,
Forget its follies and applaud its zeal.

What mines of thought they delve who backward reach
Two cycles and a half, a century each!
Even the years one human life can span,
Have almost seemed to change Creation's plan—
So full our world, so barren must have been
The fields in which our sires were wont to glean.
Trouble and hardship, danger and distress
Haunted the old Colonial wilderness,
And rose the morning sun from day to day,
Upon a bleak and almost cheerless way.
Existence was no pastime played in bowers
Of Fancy's framing decked with Fortune's flowers,
Where ugly shadows in each pathway crept,
And banished comfort even while they slept.
Pleasure was shorn of all its keenest zest,
And happiest moments were but feebly blest;
They saw not as have these—their children, seen—
A Canaan with its fields of living green,

Each hour some new-born joy or glad surprise,
And Earth reflecting gleams of Paradise.
Within the narrow circle of their lot,
They moved in line precise and faltered not,
And welcomed hardship with a joyous pride,
If but the Lord of hosts was satisfied.

Could some Van-Winkle of that Pilgrim band
Rouse from his lethargy at our command
And stalk abroad upon the city street,
Our programme of to-day had been complete:
The pen of Irving would have cried a halt,
And Jefferson's keen art have been at fault
To frame a picture of the waking dream
Of one who thus should voyage Oblivion's stream.
The swiftly passing years have wrought a change
Beyond Imagination's wildest range,
And he in veriest truthfulness might say—
"A thousand years of his were as our day."
An age of Science has affirmed its place,
And Art is pressing Nature in the race.
No longer is the restless soul content
With blessing in its crudest element,
But Life is pouring on us to the fill,
In untold measure of developed skill.
The world of art, the landscape and the field
In richer fullness of their harvests yield.
The fruits that deck our Autumn's diadem
With golden gems, were quite unknown to them;
Even the flower that by the wayside grew,
Has changed its tint and wears a lovelier hue:

From rudest plant that bloomed on sterile waste,
A dozen cultured scions charm the taste,
And fresh-born floriculture, rich and fair,
Shall greet the wakened vision everywhere.
What shall he think when even Nature moves
In paths so foreign to her old-time grooves?
With firm allegiance to the God he served,
His faith in miracles had never swerved,
But those were dimly scrolled on History's page—
A mystic record of a far-off age,
While here, beyond his senses to deny,
Are marvels wrought before his very eye.
Just for one moment bid your fancy scan
The grim and startled antiquarian:
In mournful loneliness behold him stand
A stranger in the strangest kind of land,
Who might well doubt, 'mid scenes so quaint and queer,
That ever he inhabited this sphere:
His untrained senses work as in a dream
And nineteenth-century chaos reigns supreme:
In vain the veteran stretches eyes and ears,
For some familiar sign of other years;
Was this the land that he was nurtured in—
This restless race a portion of his kin?
Could modern genius with its mighty tread,
Steal such a march above his slumb'ring head,
And progress roll in such a tidal wave,
Nor fail to start the sleeper in his grave?
And whence these wonders—from a source Divine,
Or strange devices sprung from Satan's mine?
For truly might this neophyte of ours
Suspect the working of Satanic powers,

Where every whim of daily life is hedged
By some inventive process newly fledged;—
Inventions often bearing on their face
Suspicions of a diabolic trace.
What more infernal to a casual eye
Than harnessed steam like fury dashing by,
And whence these bound unless to Pluto's realm,
Who, with some modern Stygian at the helm,
Are stalking on at such a startling speed,
Propelled by fiery breath of iron steed?
What arrant nonsense could be more complete,
Than shouts the news boy on the city street—
"Evening Gazette—last issue—all about
Some old-world king dethroned or counted out?"
Was ever stranger tale of fiction heard,
Or could be human fancy more absurd—
To hourly voice the beat of distant heart
In lands so many thousand miles apart,
And ascertain as with a lightning-flash
The daily balance of our foreign cash?
And yet, old friend, that doesn't tell it all,
For hear yon chap "hallooing" at the wall,
While every whisper that his lips convey
Is clearly listened to for miles away,
Munchausen's monstrous tales are told anew,
But modern sorcery has stamped them true;
The frozen music in his bugle-horn
No more with empty echo mocks in scorn,
Since floods of song and peal of merry laugh
Betray the secrets of the phonograph.
With every step and turn our Pilgrim takes,
Some new and strange discovery he makes;

Along the old-time lanes the street-car wheels
Press with bewildering clatter at his heels:
The wayside saplings, shorn as though by fire,
Are joined together by a web of wire,
Whose pulsing lines, as arteries of thought,
An instantaneous, world-wide voice has caught:
The tick and stroke of omnipresent clock
Salute his ear with nerve-disturbing shock;
He marked his hours, if we believe the yarn,
By chasing solar shadows round the barn,
Or if the sun for cause should fail to tell,
An hour-glass did the business quite as well.
One glance within a photographic place,
And lo! his portrait stares him in the face,
While vague remembrances of patience worn,
Struggling with sullen fire on frosty morn,
Mingled with other memories which wear
A dangerous nearness with the verb "to swear,"—
These all steal o'er him as his senses catch
Their first impressions of a friction-match.
We have a proverb held in honored trust—
"Thrice is he armed who hath his quarrel just;"
We render this upon a broader plan,
For six times armed is our revolver-man;
How old Miles Standish would have leaped for joy,
Had he possessed our military toy,
And Indian-hunting would have had a boom
To hurry many a native's day of doom.

"'Twere hard to tell which shall impress the most,—
The merits or the faults our age can boast;

As every crown is mated with a cross,
And Fate permits no gain without some loss,
So shall our newly-wakened friend find cause
To frown upon some strange and startling flaws;
Not all is gold that glitters, and, alas—
Too often flaunts its substitute in brass;
Utopia still remains a distant dream
Of inspiration for the poet's theme,
And mighty strivings for the unattained,
Leave present joys unnoticed or disdained.
The press and push of Life leave little room
For the old halcyon days of bud and bloom;
Scarce known is Youth; the infant in his pride,
Has banished cradle, and in state doth ride;
Old-fashioned childhood lingers as a myth;
Twelve-year old Jack is known as Mr. Smith;
And half-grown urchins vaunt their manhood more
Than did their ancient grandsires at four-score.
Along with lavish luxury and taste
March side by side extravagance and waste;
From Crœsus' daily meal the crumbs alone
Would make the old Thanksgiving table groan.
And God is mocked in praying for the poor
Too often hungering at the rich man's door.
Confusing customs lacking seeming sense
Crowd to the front with arrogant pretense;
Time was when honest people, it is said,
Pronounced their prayers, and tumbled into bed,
And deemed a Christian's duty fairly done
With business ended at the set of sun;
Not so with us, who entertain a freak
Which makes existence vastly more unique;

Scouting at Nature's laws, which seem to mark
Daylight for business, and for sleep the dark :
We paralyze old customs and dragoon
The work of morning into afternoon :
Thus, paradoxical, our matinee
Puts in its claim the latter half of day ;
The proper dinner is an evening rout,
And supper crowds to-morrow's breakfast out,
Disturbing habits by tradition fixed,
And rendering morn and eve a little mixed ;
Hence doth our Pilgrim find the streets at night
Aglow with modern-born electric light,
Whose spectral rays glare at him as the ghosts
Of fallen stars on lofty hitching posts.

'Tis not the province of the bard to dwell
Whereon the orator might better tell,
But sundry notions of "Ye olden time,"
Inspire a passing comment from our rhyme.
We read that "should the Governor-elect
Throw that high office into disrespect
By non-acceptance, when the public voice
Through vote unanimous declared their choice,
Due cause for declination he must show
Or pay a fine of twenty pounds or so."
Let modern statesmen ruminate on that,
When next they pass their office-seeking hat ;
With contrite heart look back upon an age
When politicians scrambled not for wage,
And when desire for high position had
Small charm to lure your Puritanic dad.

If Governors were priced at twenty pounds,
What limit, think you, of financial bounds
Would circumscribe, at proper market rate,
Some of our minor officers of state,—
Whose Titan struggles for official loaves,
Would strip the laurels from a dozen Joves?

Among old penalties for slips from grace,
We find this pointer stares us in the face;—
Shirking church service cost the absentee
In form of fine, a round ten-shilling fee.
From this small straw we find the truth evolved
Concerning one old problem long unsolved;
Why those grim saints should take such keen delight
In service, morning, afternoon and night,
Was never quite apparent till we read
The old colonial statutes on that head,
For, facts and premises brought down to us,
We reasoned to a fair conclusion thus—
If we, whose Sabbath homes are all aglow
With every comfort that a soul can know,
And piety by dint of fashion's aid,
Combines devotion with a dress-parade,—
Where inspiration generates in style,
Within some gorgeous architectural pile,
Upon whose sunlit panes the artist paints
His grotesque fancies of the honored saints,
(Creating pictures, which to unschooled eyes
Are those of angels in extreme disguise)—
With more than kind provision made for those,
Who wish religion mingled with repose,—

The studied comfort of luxuriant pews,
Where rhyme and reason both suggest a snooze,
While padded floors as flowery beds of ease,
Turn most invitingly to bended knees,
With cultured choir, who render in their *strains*,
All shades of meaning which that noun contains;—
And last, though not by any means the least,
The easy eloquence of gifted priest,
Whose rarely used anathemas are hurled
With much discretion at the outside world,
Thereby implying that his favored flock
Are no prospective part of Satan's stock,
If all this panoply of Christian art
Wake not devotion in the modern heart,
What strange inducement, human or divine
Compelled attendance at the Pilgrim's shrine?
Surely, not comfort lured the devotee
In paths, where, plainly, comfort could not be,
Nor could the ancient preacher's threatening tones
Bring balm of soothing to the sinner's groans;
The charm of music held but little part,
And e'en that little seldom reached high art,
Where voices unattuned launched into song
And dragged all shades of melody along.
But here the record haply solves the doubt
And lets a long mysterious secret out;
Who questions that a moderate fine to-day
Might guide and keep us in the better way,
And just the faintest touch of sacrifice
Develop light for our beclouded eyes?
Is there not danger that the Christian song—
"Salvation's free," is pitched a little strong,

As each one knows that what he values most
Is so esteemed with some regard to cost?

Another freak of Pilgrim enterprise
Forbade those Sabbath saints to close their eyes,—
The which was judged a pious breach of peace,
To be reported to the town police.
The old police at times were busy men,
If sermons now are types of sermons then;
And this stirs up a point we wish to state,—
That naps in church are subjects for debate:
Why should the pulpit 'scape its proper due
And all the odium fall upon the pew?
Cause and effect as equal factors pose,
Which quite explains the wearied layman's doze.
And he who cannot keep his flock awake
May fairly rate his calling a mistake.

Ah, well, the wayward world must have its joke
Though souls are weary and though hearts be broke;
Tis well to banish carking care awhile,
And solace sorrow with a sunny smile.
Pleasure and pain are proper counterparts—
A twin-born heritage of human hearts,
And whether sadness shrouds us with its spell,
Joy has its compensating claims as well.
Life lacks in flavor did we not admit
The sauce of humor and the spice of wit.
And if our Pilgrim fathers seldom smiled
Or merrily their weary hours beguiled,
Then do their virtues claim a brighter hue,
Reflected through an atmosphere so blue.

Methinks our age in this has wiser grown
And taken on a better, healthier tone;
No longer is the solemn phiz a sign
Of any kinship to a life divine,
Nor do funereal features guarantee
Their owner's conscience altogether free;
Even the parson airs his pun with grace
And smiles adorn the worthy deacon's face;
Dramatic art, so long beneath the ban,
No longer horrifies the Puritan;
And Shakespeare's shadows—(or Lord Bacon's—which?)
Are flitting almost in the cloister's niche.

It were an easy task to jog along
In simple verse and never-ending song;
The brain revolves as doth a school-boy's top,
And once in motion scarce knows when to stop.
Hour after hour the Muse might ramble on
Amid the shadows of the days agone,
And newer thoughts and fresher fancies still
Would throng Imagination's path at will:
Vast is the theme and worthy of the pen
Of loftiest flight among the poet-ken:
If but a master hand might press the keys
That chime our rich heroic harmonies,
Bringing the glories of the Past to view
In tints which I, poor limner, cannot do
Then were a picture drawn so grandly fair,
That all the world with pride its fame might share;
But I must deem my tribute fittest paid
Through thought unspoken and with word unsaid,

Content am I to chant in lighter lays
And wake the echoes of more peaceful days.

Nor were our genealogic jubilee
Complete unless we climb the family tree
And greet those scions who have held aloof
So many years from the maternal roof;
For Taunton was a mother-town, forsooth,
With wayward children in their earlier youth,
Who needs must fold their tents and, Arab-like,
For fresher fields and newer pastures strike,
And in their fond conceit to go alone,
Must set up little townships of their own,
Around the hearthstone of their childhood's home,
They need no welcome, bidding them to come,
For in the free and easy reach of all,
Our latchstring hangs upon the outer wall;
The mother-heart in self-complacent mood,
Has only plaudits for her wandering brood
And grants them, with no small degree of pride,
A place of honor by the parent's side.

Perchance, when two more centuries shall have flown
And with the Past our Present shall be known,
Our children's children with their speech and song
Shall meet and pass these compliments along;
With rev'rent hand shall take the volume down,
Which tells the story of the grand old town,
While we, as Pilgrims of a later age,
Shall furnish copy for the second page.
And will they, think you, as our names are told,
Weave with our memories some threads of gold?

Will they in truthfulness find voice to say
As we have boasted of our sires to day?
Shall they, as we have done, a story tell,—
That for our day and age, we builded well,
Or must their bard, with fetter on his tongue,
In kindness leave our eulogy unsung?
Duty enlarges with advancing years;
Louder our call than that which reached the ears
Of those whose narrow pathway day by day,
Within the handbreadth of a circle lay;
Shall our ten talents, coined of brightest gold,
For lack of use grow dim with rust and mould,
Nor richer harvest reap than they have done,
To whom the Master trusted with but one?
And here a lesson read, you whose life toil
Has been a struggle mainly for its spoil—
You who have gathered honey all your lives
Like human bees in mercenary hives—
Who, from some chance-born height of vantage place,
Have looked not Fate but Fortune in the face—
Feeding with golden spoons from Mammon's plates,
With little thought of Earth's unfortunates,—
By so much more as Fortune's friendly smile,
Through kindly Providence hath blessed your while
Above those patient souls whose lot was cast
Within a barren and unfruitful past,
So presses with an unrelenting claim,
A call of duty which to shun is shame.
Of what avail the wealth of millionaire,
Whose days are freighted with a world of care,
If increased riches open not the door
For love and charity in greater store?

If merely counting dollars were a joy,
Then blessed indeed the banker's office boy,
Whose fortune, though it scarce conceals his rags,
Is quite the equal of old Moneybags.
The rich may live and die: what better they,
Lifeless and earth-bound, than the common clay,
And hath not Scripture, as the text is given,
Almost denied to such the hope of Heaven?
Let new-born inspiration from this hour,
Lend to your gold a more benignant power;
Break the charmed circle which has wrought this spell
Of loving wealth, not wisely, but too well,
And grant the crowning grace our city needs
To round the record of her better deeds.
Enlarge her charities and hush the sneers
That all too often smite our tingling ears;
With liberal hand endow the sick man's home,
Within whose portals health and hope may come;
Be more than generous—be just to those
Who saved your country from your country's foes;
Spanning these many years of retrospect,
It seems a sorry and a strange neglect,
That bade those heroes in despondent mood,
No longer wait their city's gratitude;
May those who ring the next centennial bell
With happier voice than ours their story tell
Of monumental benefactions strewn
In every path where want or need is known.

But Time, which brings all mundane things to grief,
Bids me afford your patient ears relief;

Yet would I, ere I set my task aside,
Pledge the old hamlet with a loyal pride;
Forever be her memories a joy
Beyond all hostile fortune to destroy;
In hours of needed rest from toil, I find
Her charm of peacefulness exceeding kind;
The trees that shade her pleasant streets and ways,
A lingering vestige of the earlier days,
Are gladsome in the eyes of those who prize
The bounteous gifts which Nature's hand supplies;
The fields o'er which I rambled when a lad,
Then only with the simplest verdure clad,
Have laid aside their coat of native green,
And happy home-life paints anew the scene;
Those modest cottage-homes and garden-plots
Are more than brown-stone fronts and city lots.
"God made the country and man made the town,"
The scribe of poesy hath written down,
And though both town and country God hath willed,
And each with tokens of His goodness filled,
Yet rustic Nature wears a happier face,
Than ever shone from out the market place.

Peace be within thy walls, fair home of ours,
And prospering airs possess thy sheltering bowers;
And as the coming generations ring
The changes that successive epochs bring,
May there be written, never less than now,
A fond, maternal welcome on thy brow.
As an old homestead to the wearied heart,
Of all things else remains a joy apart,

Reaching with outstretched hand to every son,
Though he be prodigal or prudent one,
So may this homestead of a larger kin
With Memory's echoes lure her children in.
May there be tender voices in each breeze
That waves with rustling ripple through her trees;
Sermons in every rock and stone, which preach
With more than human eloquence of speech;
Books in her lakes and brooks, whose magic lore
Charms as a loving study evermore,
And good in all that tells us Nature's truth,
Which never quite betrays the dreams of Youth,
But ever and anon lights up the path
That leads the toiler toward Life's aftermath,
And he must senseless be and dull indeed,
Who in his Autumn hours has failed to read
Among the lessons that his years have brought,
That none were plainer or more kindly taught,
Than that which writes the home that gave him birth
As one among the dearest spots on earth.

www.ingramcontent.com/pod-product-compliance
Lightning Source LLC
Chambersburg PA
CBHW020904230426
43666CB00008B/1306